D1302116

A MOTHER'S
KNOT

TRAGEDY

TO TRANSFORMATION

Dear Joyce,
May your family be
fully blessed!
Gail

GAIL R. COLEMAN

A Mother's Knot
Tragedy to Transformation

Copyright © 2013 by Gail R. Coleman
www.amothersknot.com
amothersknot@hotmail.com

Cover design, book design and layout by Jim L. Friesen

Library of Congress Control Number: 2013921566

International Standard Book Number: 978-0-9910784-0-0

Printed in the United States of America by Mennonite Press, Inc., Newton, KS, www.mennonitepress.com

Dedication

To the Lord Jesus Christ,
the Savior and Keeper of my soul.
May these words glorify and honor You.
Amen

O give thanks unto the Lord; call upon his name:
Make known his deeds among the people. Psalm 105:1

Table of Contents

Foreword

CAN ANY good or even great thing come from a personal tragedy? Often times our natural thinking will not allow us to believe that such a thing could ever happen. What you will see as you read the words of Gail Coleman is that no matter how painful a situation can become, you can come to experience these words found in scripture:

And we know that all things work together for good to them that love God, to them who are the called according to his purpose.
(Romans 8:28, KJV)

The words and stories that Gail provides in this book have special meaning to me, for I lived them with her each day. I watched as she strained under the heavy load that comes with watching your child suffer and doing so from a mother's special perspective. I was there when she would struggle with the decisions of the day and then with God's help find some glimmer of hope to continue on. I was blessed to see just how deep a mother's love can penetrate into the darkness of tragedy and with the words found on these pages, you will be blessed as well.

This book will take you through, as she tells it, "Twists, Turns and Loop the Loops". You will find yourself in tears at one turn and then a remarkable confidence in the goodness of God at another. When all is said and done, you will get to see the marvelous works of God and this is exactly what she wants you to see. You will witness the love of a sister for her broken brother, the unselfish acts of a caring community and close friends, the help that comes from perfect strangers, the caring touch of a committed medical community, and most importantly, the positive determination of a suffering boy to rise out of unthinkable tragedy to a position where an observer could only ask, "How can it be?"

Though this book has it's beginning foundation in the understanding of a mother's unique connection to the suffering of her child, I can assure you as a father, you will also understand the deep pain and enjoy the moments of triumph that only a father can fully define and then say with the Psalmist

I will praise thee, O Lord, with my whole heart;
I will shew forth all thy marvelous works.
(Psalm 9:1, KJV)

Chris Coleman

Acknowledgements

I WOULD like to first and foremost thank my wonderful Savior, Christ the Lord, for saving me and loving me unconditionally. Without Him this book would never have been written.

My family deserves so much credit for reading and rereading my rough drafts, helping me to remember the sequence of events, and their patience during the month it took me to write this. Brandon gave me direction on what, and what not, to share. My mother-in-love, Ruth, and my daughter-in-love, Tammy, always gave wonderful words of encouragement. My husband, Chris, patiently took the time to read each chapter and offer suggestions. Renelle cheered me on as well. Without them I would not have had the stamina to stay with the task. I thank them and love them with my whole heart!

It was in bible study that this idea was born. The ladies that I meet with weekly suggested that I write a book. I laughed, and went home and sat down to see if I could actually make it happen. Once I started, I couldn't stop. They prayed for me every week, asked how it was going every week, and encouraged me, every week! I admire their faithfulness! Donna Adee, herself an author, helped me get started by offering suggestions and answered many questions for me. Without her wisdom, I would have been lost. I am so grateful the Lord put her in my life at such a time as this! Bianca, Connie, Donna B, Naomi, Kay, Wanda, Yvonne, LaVonne, Annabelle, Vernita, and mom prayed with me and for me all the way through this process. Their encouragement has meant so much and I thank them for believing in me and for taking me before His throne in prayer. There is no greater love than that.

I had many other friends and family encouraging me along the way. Sandy, Shannon, Brenda, Rhonda, Debbie, Regina, Teresa, Jody and Tracey, thank you for cheering me on! Melodye Hathaway, author, also gave me many suggestions, ideas and encouragement along the way.

I am so blessed with many wonderful friends. Thank you for being you, and for being a part of my life!

That Morning

May 18, 1999

IT WAS 4 a.m. I rubbed my eyes and looked again. Yup, the clock radio read 4 a.m. Ugh, why was I awake so early? Then it hit me! Brandon, my firstborn and only son, was leaving early to work out of town.

He had to be at work at 5 a.m. for his current job, and then he would get to do what he had wanted to do for a long time.

He would start his new job. *His new job!* The job he'd been waiting for so long—a job that was going to pay a lot more than minimum wage.

He would be doing maintenance work for a property leasing company—painting, fixing doorknobs and screen doors, as well as mowing. He was super excited about the future possibilities. He was thrilled just thinking about the many different ways he could spend all that money! Remember how things were when you were seventeen? Life was just about to begin and you were the master of your destiny, the captain of your very own ship!

Brandon would be graduating from high school the next spring and the possibilities were endless. I knew he was excited about his future because he had been telling me about his plans.

The very first thing on his list was to buy a *crotch rocket.* He had to explain to me what that was. (In case you didn't know, it's one of those lay-on-the-gas-tank-to-drive kind of motorcycles.) This totally horrified me! I despise *murdercycles.* That's what I call those dangerous forms of transportation. No son of mine was going to have one of those! Not without a lot of discussion. I would tell him horror stories of accidents I'd seen and some I'd heard about but to no avail, he still thought he needed one. However, I planned to make it very difficult for him. It was not going to be easy!

And then he told me of his worst plan of all. He planned to move out after graduation! Ouch, I wasn't ready to hear that one! We would definitely be discussing that one!

As I lay there in bed thinking about all his plans and his enthusiasm, I heard him downstairs rustling around, getting ready for work. I made my way down the stairs to find him already dressed and ready to go. His king size water bed was all strewn with bedding and clothes and who knows what else. He would straighten it all up when he had the chance or when I would remind him to do it. Seventeen-year olds need lots of reminders.

I just had to stop a minute and realize how he had grown. He was no longer my little boy, but was becoming a man. He was 6'4", 180 pounds and very mature and responsible for his age. Somehow my heart was heavy, burdened. I asked him all the questions mothers ask, "Are you coming home for lunch?"

"No, I'll grab a bite somewhere."

"What time do you start?"

"I clock in at 1 p.m."

"Do you have enough gas?"

"Yes, Mom." He rolled his eyes.

I wanted to hold on to him and keep him my little boy and was somewhat irritated that he didn't have a need for me to be his mommy anymore. But something even deeper was troubling me, but I couldn't quite put my finger on it. It was that Mother's Knot in the gut that appears from time to time.

I kissed him good-bye and told him to be careful. It was still quite dark, and there were a lot of deer in the area. I reminded him to keep an eye out for them, just in case one decided to dart out in front of him. I got another roll of the eyes. Then I wished him a good day and hoped his first day at his new job went well.

I watched out the front room window as he backed out of the driveway with that old pick-up that he had bought from his Uncle Keith for a dollar.

The blue pickup with the handmade wooden bed sitting next to our house.

I had to admire all the work he had put into it. He had taken the rusted old bed off and built a flat bed out of lumber that he purchased with his own money. Admittedly, when he first told me of this plan, I thought it would look rather cheesy, but I have to say, he did a great job on it. I was so proud of him. As I watched him drive away, I prayed for him. I prayed for his safety traveling and I prayed that he would like his new job. But yet, there was still this nagging in my soul. I prayed again that his day would be blessed by God and that He would protect him.

I made the coffee and soon my husband Chris was up getting ready for work. Then right after him, Renelle, my baby girl was up too. Well, she wasn't a baby anymore. She would be graduating from the 8th grade in a couple of weeks. I kissed Chris good bye as he rushed out the door and Renelle and I had breakfast together.

As we ate we were discussing how to spend our summer once school was out. I had mentioned to the kids that I would like to find something meaningful and educational to do with our summer. A home missions project, or helping someone in need with home repairs or yard work or taking day trips to see historical sites or museums—something life-changing or inspirational. I wanted something to make an impact on our children's future that would give them motivation for what they wanted to spend their life doing. I had always dreamed of some kind of ministry or mission work. Brandon had expressed at one time as a young child that he wanted to be a missionary pilot and take missionaries into deep forests and far away hidden places.

After the breakfast dishes were done, Renelle got started on her homework and I on my housework. We homeschooled, and it was always the first thing on the agenda for the day. I enjoyed spending time and learning with the kids. I believe I learned more homeschooling than I did when I went to school.

It was lunch time before we knew it. The phone rang and it was Brandon. He called to let me know that he had had lunch, pizza with some friends. He had a good morning and was headed to his new job. Ah, he was safe, all was well. I was so glad that he called to let me know. It was 12:45 p.m. He would be starting his new job in fifteen minutes! I was anxious and excited for him! We had raised our children to always work as though God was their boss. Never do anything halfway, always do more than expected, be honest, and to remember that *not* working while you are clocked in is actually stealing from your employer. I knew Brandon would be an excellent employee for his new boss. He had already demonstrated those qualities with previous employers.

After lunch I went to do the ironing in my sewing room. It was a Tuesday, and that is ironing day. The ironing board was in front of the east window that faced the houses across the street. Then behind those houses flowed Sand Creek. It was a beautiful sunny day and somehow ironing in front of that window, while it was open, almost felt like I was enjoying the outdoors.

I still had this great burden to pray for Brandon. I wasn't sure what I was to pray for, but his safety kept coming to my mind. So as I ironed I was conversing with the Lord, and I believe at times it was even audible! I was so adamant that the Lord hear me and answer my prayer. I began praying about Brandon's desire to buy a crotch rocket and telling the Lord that he is almost a man and I don't have much influence in his decisions anymore. If I was to give him my blessing to purchase one, (as if he would wait for that) could

I live with it if he were killed in an accident? Could I live with it if he killed someone while driving it? Could I live with it if he were permanently brain damaged or paralyzed? It was the most fervent I had ever been in my prayer time with the Lord. I could not understand it. Why was I so troubled? As I struggled with the Lord in this conversation, I had somewhat of a peace come over me. It was if I came to realize that even if these things may happen, we would still honor and glorify the Lord. Even in death or permanent damage, I would still lovingly care for him and we would still be loved and blessed by God. I couldn't imagine us ever having to deal with anything so horrible. I trusted the Lord. But that Mother's Knot was still there, that uneasy gut feeling would not go away.

A Knock at the Door

I HAD finished the ironing and Renelle and I had decided that we had a sweet tooth. So we picked out a recipe that we hadn't made in a long time: Yum Yum bars! We got the oven preheating, made the cookie bar part and put it in the pan and began the fun part, beating egg whites until stiff. This always seemed to take so long, so we took turns holding the hand mixer, when there was a knock at the door. It was about 3:30 in the afternoon.

I went to the front door, opened it, and there stood a young police officer with a very serious look on his face. My first thought was whether my neighbors were OK. Were they looking for a suspect on the loose in our neighborhood? What could it possibly be?

"Are you Mrs. Coleman?" he asked.

"Yes," my heart was racing.

"Your son's been in an accident." His words did a slow motion replay in my ears.

I immediately felt sick, almost dizzy. Time stopped. I couldn't breathe. I had just talked to Brandon two hours ago and he was fine!

"In his truck?" My heart sank. I pictured his blue pickup smashed on Highway 50 somewhere. My fingers went numb.

"No ma'am, in Sand Creek."

"Sand Creek?" I asked. "His truck went in Sand Creek?" I pictured it crashing through the rail and plunging into the water off the 12th Street Bridge.

"No, on his lawn mower," he said. Brandon was using a hydrostatic mower that was big and tall and lever-controlled. At the time I was unaware of this, so I couldn't picture it. I could only picture a push mower and that didn't make sense.

At that instant I looked up past the officer's shoulder and across the street behind our neighbor's houses where Sand Creek is. I could see people in the distance, lots of people, standing on the sidewalk that runs along the creek on the opposite side.

I pointed in that direction and asked the young officer, "Over there where those people are?"

"Unfortunately, yes."

I reached my hand out to hold his, for stability, I needed him to hold me up.

"Is he OK?" I asked.

"He's alive, and they are working on him."

"They are working on him? What does that mean? Can I go over there?" I wanted to know.

"Well, I don't know if I would recommend it, but yes," he answered reluctantly.

I thanked him and turned to go back in the house and he turned to leave. Renelle was standing behind me and I said, "Brandon's in Sand Creek, I have to go over there!" She'd heard the whole conversation.

"I'll go with you," she said.

We ran together across the street, into the back yards along the creek, and about three houses down Renelle said, "Should I go back and call Daddy?"

"Oh yeah, good idea," I said breathlessly. Why didn't I think of that? My mind was swirling.

I continued running and watching the people on the riverbank and people on the sidewalk across the creek. And they were watching and pointing at me. I couldn't see Brandon yet, but I continued to run and pray. This time I was praying for Brandon's life. They were working on him, working on him how? I couldn't run fast enough to be by his side to see if he was OK. I hoped that he knew I loved him and that I was on my way. The ground was uneven and I didn't have the best shoes on for running, but somehow I just kept my speed up and my shoes on.

I saw the first responders, EMTs, and police officers standing on the edge of the embankment. The embankment was 12 to 15 feet above the creek and I walked over to where I could see they were busy doing something, I couldn't tell what. I looked over the edge and saw an EMT sitting on a ledge supporting Brandon's upper body while the rest of him floated freely in the creek. It appeared as though they were talking to each other. The other EMTs were lowering a cage-looking thing down the steep drop-off with a rope. One of the officers on the embankment told me that I needed to step away and let them work. I felt so alone, so helpless, so detached from what was happening. I didn't even know how or what to pray for. All I could say was, "Help me Lord." My entire body was shaking uncontrollably.

It seemed like forever when they finally hoisted him up the embankment. They had him in a neck brace, on a back board and in this cage-looking stretcher. I ran over to him, looked down into his face and Brandon said, "I'm gonna be OK, Mom." The relief that hit me nearly made my knees buckle. To be able to see his eyes and hear his voice was so reassuring. There was no blood, except for a scratch on his leg, and to look at him, he looked fine! I cried. I had no words. I was just so thankful that he was alive.

By now Chris and Renelle had arrived on the scene and the EMTs were getting ready to load Brandon into the ambulance. They offered to let one of us ride along, and it had to be me. I couldn't stand to not be with my baby. So Chris and Renelle followed us in the car. We drove to the next city, about thirty minutes away, because they had much bigger hospitals and trauma units. The lights and sirens were wailing. I looked back to see the EMT making marker lines on Brandon's chest, asking him if he could feel it.

"Is he paralyzed?" I asked.

"He is showing signs of paralysis, but it may not be permanent, we don't know yet." He said.

All of a sudden I felt I was going to throw up. I told the driver, "I think I'm gonna be sick."

"It's shock, that's normal. There is a barf bag in that compartment in front of you if you need it," he kindly offered.

I reached in and took it out, but I hate throwing up. It would have been so embarrassing and the last thing I wanted anyone to do was take care of me. So I sat back, took some deep breaths, closed my eyes and asked God to help me not be sick. I needed to be OK for Brandon's sake. The nausea passed.

I was amazed as we drove how many people didn't stop or move over to let us through. I asked the driver if this was normal for them to have to deal with and he said, "Oh yeah, people don't follow the rules anymore. We have to be extra cautious because you never know when someone may pull out right in front of you."

I always pulled over for emergency vehicles before, but I do even more so now. When you have a loved one being rushed to the hospital, you value the importance of letting emergency vehicles have the right of way!

We arrived at the hospital and Brandon was whisked away to the trauma unit and Chris, Renelle and I were led to the waiting area—the dreaded waiting area, where they have you sit and know absolutely nothing about what is going on for what seems like hours. We paced the floor and looked for someone with any information. Finally someone arrived to tell us what is going on.

"They've taken your son to prep for surgery," she said.

"What kind of surgery?" I ask.

"Your son has a shattered C-6 vertebra. They will remove the shattered pieces of bone, take a piece of donated bone from the bone bank to make him a new vertebra, insert it in its place and then take a metal plate and screws and fuse C-5, C-6 and C-7 together. It will make his neck stronger than it's ever been," she said.

I was still trying to accept the fact that my son had a broken neck, let alone understand what a C-6 vertebra was. I didn't fully comprehend what was happening. I couldn't imagine him having a broken neck. Does this mean he's paralyzed? They never said anything about that. But I remembered the marker lines on his chest from the ambulance ride. They were very high on his chest. Quadriplegia? Immediately I thought of Superman, Christopher Reeves, in his wheelchair on a ventilator to help him breathe. This couldn't be happening to us. Not our son!

"Is he paralyzed?" I didn't really want to know the answer, but I had to ask.

"He is showing paralysis, but if we get the pressure off of his spinal cord he could get his feeling back. We just don't know yet." She sounded hopeful.

"You can go in to see him before they take him into surgery. He is hypothermic so we have him in a cocoon-like thing that is filled with hot air to warm his body up before the surgery," she informed us.

Someone led us to the surgical prep room and there he was in the cocoon. I could hear my heartbeat. He was awake, but not very coherent. We prayed for him. We cried. How was he going to emerge from that cocoon? Was he going to be whole? How could this be happening to our son? It was so hard to leave his side and put him in the hands of the surgeon. I realized that I was no longer in control of anything in Brandon's life. I had to totally surrender him to God, and trust Him to take care of him. And after all, doesn't He love Brandon more than I do anyway?

We made our way back to the waiting room and several people from our Home School Support Group and from our church were there. Mom and Keith, Chris' brother, had arrived and we all waited and prayed together. Even with a room full of friends and family, I still felt very alone. Afraid. I didn't even know how to pray. I knew the Lord knew it all. It was around 6 or 7 p.m.

After a four hour surgery the surgeon finally appeared. He was removing the mask from his face as he walked toward us. Somehow I wanted to walk away, I didn't want to hear what he was going to say, but I had to know. How was Brandon, how did the surgery go? He explained the surgery to us, how they inserted the donated piece of hip bone into the C-6 location, screwed in a plate and stitched him back up. The surgery went well and Brandon did fine through it all. Now for the difficult question, "Is he...paralyzed?" The surgeon looked less than hopeful.

"There is considerable bruising to the spinal cord. When his head hit the bottom of the creek, the impact shattered the C-6 vertebra forcing it into his spinal cord." He used his fingers to demonstrate and the picture became very clear. "A person can break his neck and not be paralyzed. It's when the spinal cord is affected that the paralysis occurs. And there is definite bruising on his cord at the C-5, C-6 and C-7 level. In most cases when someone is instantly paralyzed, it is usually permanent," he said sadly.

We didn't know what to say, or what to ask. We stood there...speechless. He said he was sorry—he did all he could do. He told us not to lose hope. "So there was still hope?" It sure didn't feel like it. All I could feel was a sick, weak-kneed sensation, and my heart was breaking for my son.

They moved Brandon into surgical ICU, showed us to that waiting room, and instructed us that one or two of us could see him at ten minutes before the hour, each hour, but that was it. Visitation was limited. I couldn't wait to get to see him. What was I going to tell him? Should I tell him yet? Would he be awake enough? How do you tell your 17-year old son that he may be paralyzed for life? I couldn't accept it. God had to have a plan, a plan to heal him in some miraculous way! That was it. God would heal him and be glorified! I had to believe that. I wanted everyone to believe that.

We went to into the recovery room and saw the bandages on his throat. They had done the surgery from the front and Brandon was still very asleep. It was a very small incision, only an inch or two. We prayed over him and headed back to the waiting room. It must have been around midnight by then.

Many people had come to the hospital to see how he was doing. A friend from my mom's *In Touch* prayer group, Debbie, had run back to our house to check on things. She said she turned the oven off (it was still on for the Yum Yum bars), cleaned up the kitchen, and said that the mixer was in this bowl with some kind of yucky looking white stuff. It was the egg whites. They had lost their stiffness and were unidentifiable. Our dog Tippy was in desperate need of a trip outdoors, so she tended to her as well. She locked up the house for us and she also thought to grab my Bible and the devotional books that were with it. She said it was such an eerie picture to step into my kitchen and to see how life had stopped. It felt like life had stopped. Like the clock shouldn't be ticking. I was so grateful she thought of all of that, because it hadn't crossed my mind at all.

Soon everyone left, including Renelle. She went to stay with her friend, Ashley. Mom, Chris and I made make-shift recliners with two chairs in the waiting room to try and close our eyes for a rest, but that wasn't very comfortable. We lay down on the floor, but it was too hard. We were so restless, yet exhausted, however sleep was not to be found. We would just sit awake, discussing the what-ifs, how-comes, and what-nows. We found comfort in each other and were waiting at the door every hour for our ten minute visit with Brandon, even though he was unaware that we were there.

The Roller Coaster

I HAVE a love/hate relationship with roller coasters. When driving into the amusement park and looking in awe at the height of the steep inclines and drops of those crazy things, I can feel my adrenalin increase, and I get butterflies in my stomach at the very thought of riding on one. Then as I walk up to it, stand in line for it, and watch other riders getting off of it, I begin to have second thoughts. Hmmm, this ride doesn't look like something I can do after all, because I am scared of heights. Maybe I'll take the chicken exit? But then again, I don't want everyone to laugh at me, call me a baby, and "braawwk" at me like a chicken. I really do want to experience the thrill and the fear of the ride! So I get on, make sure my seatbelts are very secure and hang on for the ride. The whole time I'm saying to myself, "Why did I get on this thing?" "Somebody help me!" "If I live through this, I will never ride another one ever again!" And I scream all the way up, and all the way down, and on every turn! Brandon told me once that he never wanted to sit with me again on a roller coaster! It hurt his ears to have to listen to me! But, it was so fun, even if I did scream the whole time!

What I soon came to realize was that our journey through ICU would become the most horrifying roller coaster ever experienced. It all started the second day. The sun came up and the lights came back on in the waiting room. I opened my devotional book to get a word from the Lord. I needed Him more now than I ever did. I wanted to know what His plan was for Brandon. Why did He allow this to happen? Was He really in control? But I knew He was there. He did not leave us, nor forsake us. But why?

As I am writing this today, I went back and reread those particular devotionals. It sent a chill up my spine and covered me with goose bumps. I just have to share them with you. The first one I read comes out of *Our Daily Bread* from RBC ministries. The title was "The Rescue." The title grabbed my attention right away. This is what I read the morning after the accident, the underlining is mine:

The psalmist told us that God "put a new song in my mouth—praise to our God" (Ps. 40:3). The song did not come easily to him. *"He…brought me up out of a horrible pit,"* he testified, *"out of the miry clay, and set my feet upon a rock, and established my steps" (v.2).*

We don't know what this "pit" was. Perhaps it was *a devastating calamity,* or the result of a willful, ungodly choice. In either case, it was horrible. *The place was unspeakably lonely, as silent as death, and he could find no solid place to put his feet. He couldn't climb out of "the miry clay" by himself. It took God to rescue him.*

A Chinese scholar who converted to Christ told this parable: "A man fell into a dark, dirty pit, and he tried to climb out but he couldn't. Confucius came along. He saw the man in the pit and said, 'Poor fellow. If he had listened to me, he never would have fallen in.' And he left. Buddha came along and saw the man in the pit and said, 'Poor fellow. If he can climb up here, I'll help him.' And he too left. *Then Christ came and said, 'Poor fellow!' And He jumped into the pit and helped him out."*

God rescued the psalmist from the "pit." And He gave him a new song to sing, which we too can sing if we've experienced God's deliverance from trouble.

> *He took me out of the miry clay,*
> *He set my feet on the rock to stay,*
> *He put a song in my soul today,*
> *A song of praise, hallelujah!–Anon.*

God's dawn of deliverance often comes when the hour of trial is darkest.

We almost laughed out loud. I know you are thinking, "Really? You laughed?" We hadn't slept in twenty-four hours and we really needed a word from the Lord, so it was pure joy when we read that! It was so fitting, so perfect. We knew God lifted him out of the muddy Sand Creek and rescued him. Then we picked up *My Utmost For His Highest* by Oswald Chambers. This is a much more difficult read, but very deep thinking. The title of this one was: "Out of the Wreck I Rise"! How could this be? Did Someone plant these in my books? It reads:

"Who shall separate us from the love of Christ?" Romans 8:35

"Never let cares or tribulations separate you from the fact that God loves you."

God does not keep a man immune from trouble; He says— "I will be with him in trouble." It does not matter what actual troubles in the most extreme form get hold of a man's life, not one of them can separate him from his relationship to God.

"Shall tribulation...?" Let tribulation be what it may—*exhausting, galling,* it is not able to separate us from the love of God. Never let cares or tribulations separate you from the fact that God loves you.

Either Jesus Christ is a deceiver and Paul is deluded, or *some extraordinary thing happens to a man who holds on to the love of God when the odds are against God's character. Logic is silenced in the face of every one of these things. Only one thing can account for it—the love of God in Christ. "Out of the wreck I rise" every time.*

WOW. We just sat back in awe. The Lord had definitely spoken to us that morning in the waiting room. He would never leave us or forsake us, He would be with us in trouble, and He lifted Brandon out of the miry clay and set his feet upon a rock. He was in control, and we had a renewed assurance.

Later that morning several people arrived to find out how Brandon was doing. It was overwhelming the amount of support, encouragement, and love that we were shown! We had only lived in the area nine months so we weren't total strangers, but we weren't hometown kids either. Some people who came I had never even met. One lady came up to me and asked me if I was the boy's mom?

I said, "Yes, Brandon is my son."

"I saw the whole thing." She said, still shook up. "I was sitting in the drive-thru at McDonalds and I could see him mowing across the creek on that high embankment. I don't know if he lost control of that big mower or what, but the mower fell off the edge and your son screamed as he dove, head first into the creek." I could tell she was shaking. "I don't know how to swim, so I couldn't help him, so I ran into the store and told everyone that a boy went off the cliff with his mower and he was still in the water. So a man who was in the store went into the water and pulled him out. I never want to witness anything like that again in my life! I sure hope he's going be OK?"

I put my hand on her shoulder and said," We hope so too!" "I'm so glad you were there and that you called for help. Thank you!" I asked her if she'd like to see Brandon and she shook her head, "No, I just needed to tell you what I saw." I thanked her again and she turned to leave.

Another official looking lady approached me and asked to speak with me privately. She led me to a quiet hallway and explained that we had options on how all of this was going to be paid for. I had never even given a thought to the cost, yet!

"You do know that you have every right to sue don't you?" she asked.

"Well, we aren't the suing kind. And if this was just an accident, of Brandon losing control of the mower, I don't see any reason to sue." I said, not really knowing what I was talking about.

"Well, you still have grounds for a lawsuit. However, if you let worker's compensation handle it all, Brandon will be taken care of for the rest of his life. You may receive a very substantial settlement if you choose to sue, but there's no way of knowing all the expenses your son may accrue in his lifetime. You could run out of money a lot sooner than you might think possible in a situation like this."

"No, I'm sure we don't have any desire to sue. Worker's comp sounds like the answer for us."

She shook my hand and said if I ever had any questions she would be glad to help.

Then came a man and he introduced himself as Vern. He said, "I'm the one that helped Brandon get out of the water."

"You are?" I said, "Thank you so much! What happened?" I asked.

"I was sitting in McDonald's having coffee with the guys at 3:00 p.m. like I always do on Tuesdays, and a lady comes running into the store yelling, 'Someone call 911. A boy just drove his mower off the cliff, and he's not getting up out of the water!' So we jumped up and ran outside to see what was happening." He said, "I could see the wheels of the big mower sticking out of the water, and a few feet away I could see this young man's head bobbing up and down, but he wasn't getting out of the water. I thought to myself, there ain't no way that boy's gonna make it till the ambulance gets here."

"I looked around at all of us standing on the sidewalk watching, but none of us was doing anything! People from inside Wendy's, McDonalds and Taco Bell were all standing out there watching. So I took off my shoes, and took my wallet out of my pocket, why I took the time to do that I don't know, but I got in the creek and waded across about twenty feet to where he was. It was only hip deep at the deepest point, and maybe two and a half feet deep where Brandon was. I took a hold of his head and shoulders and rolled him over, and he said, 'Thanks man!' He didn't cough out any water at all! And then do you know what he said to me? He said, 'Tell my boss I'll pay him for the mower.' I couldn't believe that this kid was at all concerned about that lawn mower. I told him don't you worry about that lawn mower. I gently pulled him over to the ledge and held him and waited for the EMTs. He was so calm. I couldn't get over how calm he was. He was even cracking jokes! I think I was more scared than he was! He had to be underneath that water at the very least four minutes, and he never lost consciousness. That's just amazing!"

I hugged him, I cried. I thanked him for saving Brandon's life!

From that moment on Vern Whitesell has been my superhero. Anyone who would take the chance and help one of my loved ones in distress will always be a superhero in my book! I took him in to see Brandon, and Brandon thanked him again for helping him out of the water. I hugged him again, and every time I see him, I hug him and his wife. I wish there was some way I could pay him back. There isn't enough money in the world to pay for what he did in saving Brandon.

This is my superhero on the right, Vern Whitesell, and his lovely wife Norma on the left.

Later that same day the neurosurgeon called us into a small room and sat us down. She began to explain the details of Brandon's condition. She said that he was a C-5, 6 quadriplegic. That he would live out his life in a wheelchair and probably need assistance with basic tasks. I felt as though I was listening in on a conversation that she was having with someone else. I looked around the room, but no, it was just us. She was telling this tragic news to us! I asked if there was any hope for a full recovery and she explained that when paralysis happens instantly in an accident, it is usually permanent. However, there is a two-year window that some function could be regained. Those were the only words that I clung to. Two years. Could God work a miracle in two years? Yes, he could! He could heal him tomorrow if He chose to! I would hold on to that hope. I wasn't ready to accept anything less. My son didn't deserve this.

Brandon was doing well recovering from his surgery, still groggy somewhat, but his vitals were all good. So good in fact that they decided he could go to a regular room! They needed his bed in ICU for a more critical patient. We were so shocked and relieved that he was recovering so quickly! It had only been twenty four hours since his surgery. A regular room? On a regular floor? No tubes or wires, no nurse in constant attendance? We were almost thrilled! We wouldn't have limited visitation. We could see him as long as we wanted to. This had to be a good sign. I could see home in our very near future! We had been so busy with visitors, and delirious from no sleep that we didn't even recognize that we had just climbed the steep incline of the roller coaster and we were at the summit getting ready to take the big plunge.

The Big Plunge

BRANDON HAD a great love for basketball. And he was good! He would go to the Rec Center everyday at noon to play pick-up basketball with the men that would show up and then he'd return home to pick up his sister Renelle, and they would spend the afternoon playing with other kids from the home school group. It was a great way for them to get their exercise and spend time with friends. It was also a good leverage tool to get assignments done! If work wasn't completed, no basketball. When he was a junior he could dunk, and he had dreams of being a walk-on at one of our state universities. He taught Renelle to play too, and both of them were good and so fun to watch.

Because he was in such good shape physically, he was recovering well. All of his vitals remained steady throughout this time. However, while we were in the process of moving him, a woman came up to Chris' mom, Ruth, in the waiting room and asked her if she was related to Brandon. When Mom said, "Yes, I'm his grandmother," she then put her hand over her hospital name tag and said, "I am coming to you as someone who is concerned for Brandon's condition. I am a speech pathologist and I don't feel that Brandon is ready to be moved to a regular room. His evaluation revealed that he isn't able to swallow, cough or clear his throat yet, so I don't think he should be left alone. I recommend someone stay in that room with him tonight. Don't leave him alone for even a second."

When we all got to Brandon's new room Mom told us of this conversation that she had with this woman. We found it odd that no one else had warned us about this, and we weren't even sure why, but we followed her advice and Chris stayed in the room with him.

We were so relieved that Brandon was doing so well, even though he still couldn't move. We decided to get a motel room down the street to see if we could get some sleep. Mom and I would go sleep for a few hours and then trade places with Chris. We kissed Chris and Brandon good-night and headed up the street. After we got checked in we climbed into bed and immediately we were asleep.

All of a sudden the phone rang. It hadn't been thirty minutes since we got there.

"Brandon had a code blue and they're taking him back to ICU!" Chris said.

"Why? What happened?" Panic set in.

"He aspirated and stopped breathing!" I could hear the fear in Chris' voice.

Immediately Mom and I were dressed, and we hurried back to the hospital and back to the ICU waiting room where Chris was waiting. "He's going be OK. They put him on a ventilator."

A ventilator? My son, who was recovering so well, was now on a ventilator? How did this happen? Why?

Chris explained that Brandon had been begging for a drink

of water because his mouth and his throat were so dry. It was way beyond cottonmouth, it was painfully dry. It was painful for him to move his tongue or lips or even try to swallow. So he kept asking the nurse for something, anything to help moisten his mouth. She told him he wasn't allowed water to drink but she would bring him some ice chips. Since Brandon was unable to move his arms, Chris would rub the ice over his lips and his tongue to moisten them.

They were sitting there watching TV when Brandon said, "I feel like I can't breathe." So Chris jumped up and leaned Brandon over to the side to see if that would help him catch his breath, when all of a sudden Chris noticed that Brandon had stopped breathing! Immediately Chris hit the button and ran to the hall for help! The nurse came in and Chris said, "He's not breathing!" The nurse says, "Oh he's fine." Chris is insistent, " No, see, he is *not* breathing!" She looked closer and then called for a code blue. Before long the room was full of doctors and nurses and Chris was in the hall waiting...hoping.

It seemed like forever before we were back in ICU and we are allowed in to see him. Our hearts sank when we saw the huge tube coming out of his mouth and the machine pumping air into his lungs. The sheer exhaustion was gone. A whole new supply of adrenalin kicked in and sleep would not be needed. The total discouragement and hopelessness was almost more than we could bear. All we could do was look at him and cry. I went to his side and held his lifeless hand wishing I could feel him squeeze mine. I cried more. I noticed more tubes and wires coming out of him. One led to a container on the wall that was full of blood. "Where is the blood coming from?" I asked the nurse. She explained that it was called an NG tube and it was coming from his stomach. He had a bleeding ulcer from the trauma of the accident and she told me not to worry; it wasn't unusual in his circumstance. I noticed a bag at the end of his bed capturing his urine—IVs in both hands, electrodes on his chest, and the tube taped to his mouth. I leaned over and kissed him on the forehead. He still had mud in his hair from the creek bottom and I noticed it in his ears and eyebrows as well. I wanted to wash it away for him. Take care of him, make him whole again. I couldn't stop crying. He was completely sedated, he looked almost dead. I couldn't even consider the thought. I could not lose my son. I thought about how he would stand face to face to me and measure

This is when Brandon began to start measuring himself against me.

This is when he finally passed me up. Chris, Renelle, and Ruth are also pictured here.

how tall he was against me. I am 6'1", and I'll never forget the joy on his face when he was as tall as me. And then the smugness he displayed when he was finally taller than me.

Would he ever do that again? Then my mind wandered to the times we'd argued, the times I would yell at him out of my impatience. I demanded such perfection from my children and left little room for willful disobedience or mistakes. Guilt wanted to take a hold of me. Why was I so hard on him? Is this my fault? Who's to blame? Someone has to be to blame right? I asked God to forgive me for all the mistakes I'd made as a mother and to please not let Brandon suffer because of me.

Our time was up. We had to leave him and go back to the waiting room. I was really beginning to get tired of that place. I wanted to be with my son. On the way back I stopped in the restroom and as soon as I was completely alone, I broke down and cried until I couldn't cry any more. I locked myself in the stall and begged God not to take my son. "Please Lord, heal his body. I need him. He's too young to die. Life is just beginning for him! Please, don't let this be because of my mistakes." After several minutes of uncontrollable crying and begging God, my mind rested on the scripture that says, "The sins of the fathers will not be visited on their children" Ezekiel 18:20. "Thank you, Lord, for reminding me of that! God does not punish our children because of our sin." The guilt was subsiding. I only wanted what was the very best for my kids. I left that stall and walked back to the waiting room to wait for our next visit. That restroom stall became my sanctuary.

Again the waiting room was packed full. Word had gotten around that Brandon took a turn for the worse and was back in ICU. We told and retold the story over and over and we never tired of telling it. It was somehow, cathartic. To have so many people there to lean on and showing their love and concern was overwhelming. We gained strength from all their support. After the day of good news and positive reports it ended in one breath-taking plunge to the bottom. And Brandon had no idea how serious it was.

Twists, Turns and Loop the Loops

FROM THAT day on, the next three weeks would be a constant up and down roller coaster ride.

And up: The local newspaper had printed a front page story about the accident and even more people came to the hospital to encourage, support and pray with us. It felt a little awkward to have everybody in town know everything about us. We had never made front page news before. But the support was very comforting. The waiting room and hallway were full of people. Those in charge of the ICU came to us and told us that they would allow five visitors at a time, for five minutes, just so the hallways could clear out. Many came to pray over Brandon and all came to offer encouragement. I believe with all my heart that God heard and answered their prayers. The number of people was overwhelming and that is an understatement.

And down: Brandon's lungs collapsed because they were full of fluid and he code blued a second time. They inserted chest tubes. First just one, but not very long after that they were inserting the second one. Brandon was awake for that one and said later that it was so strange to watch what they were doing and not be able to feel a thing. It was so scary. He now had more tubes and containers capturing fluid under his bed. I returned to my "sanctuary" and again cried out and begged God not to take my son. I reminded God that I knew that Brandon was His son first and that I knew He loved Brandon more than I did, and that I trusted Him to take care of my son.

And loop the loop: Renelle's eighth grade graduation was here. She had prepared her display boards, projects and awards. In the weeks before, we went shopping together and bought a new dress and shoes. She was ready to take the next step in her life. The struggle of wanting to be there and needing to be with Brandon was heart wrenching. I wanted so badly to cross this milestone with her, but Brandon was hanging on by a thread. I cried. I couldn't be at both places. I asked Renelle if she could forgive me for missing her graduation and she so sweetly reassured me that I needed to stay with Brandon. Daddy would be there, and Grandma too. Renelle has always been so unselfish and considerate. Definitely a sweet heart! It was another reminder that I was losing control in every area of my life. It was so hard to watch Renelle leave knowing that I was going to miss this celebration in her life. It was even harder to have her stay with friends and not be able to go home. Home was where we were, and where we were was not homey. I could not bring myself to force her to stay with us just because I wanted her with us. Living in the ICU waiting room was hard on us as adults, let alone a fourteen-year-old young lady. She was mature enough to make her own decisions about where she wanted to be, and most days, she spent with Brandon and me. Then in the evening she would stay with friends. I hated it, but couldn't do anything about it.

And up: The graduation was a great event and following the ceremony they had asked Chris to give an update on Brandon. When Chris was through sharing the updates, the auditorium full of people came forward to shake his hand, to tell him they were praying for Brandon, and to stuff money in his suit. When the room was empty Chris looked like a scarecrow! His suit was full of money that the people had given! God provided before we even knew we would have a need.

And turn: Mom's pastor and his wife felt compelled to put us up in the hotel just outside in the hospital parking lot. They would pay the bill for our entire stay of three and a half weeks. We lived on one income and money was tight. This was such a blessing! We wouldn't have to sleep in the waiting room anymore. Chris returned to work during the day and would come to the hospital when he got off in the evening. This way we would be able to stay together at night. It was always so hard to leave Brandon's side. I would have to literally make myself let go, and trust God every time I walked away from him. Each night in that hotel room we would lift Brandon up to the Lord, hold each other tight, and cry to a restful sleep.

And twist: Brandon had lost so much blood from the ulcer that he needed a blood transfusion. He would need three during his stay in ICU.

And loop the loop: A lady approached me in the waiting room and introduced herself as Pat.

She told me that she was assigned to Brandon from his employer's work comp insurance company. She was so sweet and respectful and genuinely wanted to hear the

This is our lovely God-send Pat, on the left. Chris is in the middle and me on the right.

whole story. She asked about Brandon's condition and asked permission to see him. I took her in to meet Brandon. He barely opened his eyes to acknowledge her. She introduced herself and then explained why she was there. She reassured him that he would be well taken care of. When we walked back to the waiting room, she had tears in her eyes. Her real compassion was such a sweet blessing. To know that all of his bills would be taken care of, all of his needs met, it was overwhelming. Joy and humble gratefulness filled my soul. It would be the silver lining in this black cloud, because the expenses of this injury were mountainous! We lived on one income and our budget was stretched. It seemed impossible that we would be able to afford to care for his needs. Pat was so reassuring and gave us so much peace that everything was taken care of. She was such a God-send in so many ways. She brought such encouragement on so many levels. I still thank God for her always, even though she retired years ago.

And up: On one of our visits to see Brandon he was wide awake! The most awake I had seen him in days! He was blinking his eyes at me in such a way that he was trying to tell me something. I was guessing everything I thought it could be, but continued to be wrong. Then I had a revelation! He wanted me to have the bright lights turned off. When I finally guessed it, Brandon did his usual roll of the eyes that I had seen him do many times before when he was trying to tell me something that I didn't understand, and then he gave me a very relieved nod. I laughed, no giggled with glee! I kissed him on the forehead and told him I was sorry it took me so long to get it. Brandon always had a great sense of humor, and it felt *so* good to see it! He was still my son, the son I loved.

And down: After two weeks without any food they decided to put in a feeding tube. Brandon was losing weight rapidly. It proved to be a very difficult task. They found out that his duodenum was shaped like a J instead of the more common C-shape that most people have. So when they would push the tube down his nose, through his esophagus, into his stomach and into the intestines it had a high hill to climb in that J shape. It required a very large machine, a long rod and an uncomfortable shove through the mouth, down the throat and into the stomach. Not an easy task, and fortunately for Brandon, they administered a drug that would make him forget the procedure completely.

After a few days the feeding tube became clogged. The nurses struggled to unclog it using every method they knew. On the evening shift change, I entered the room for my ten-minute visit to find a new nurse preparing to pull out the feeding tube.

"Why are you going to remove it?" I asked.

"Well, it's clogged. We can't get it unclogged, so I'm going to put a new one in."

"Oh, really?" I said. "You make it sound so easy! They had a very difficult time getting it down the other day. It required quite a procedure, due to the fact that he has a J-shaped duodenum. They said that it should *never* be removed." I informed her.

"Well, I've been a nurse for over twenty-five years, and I've inserted a lot of feeding tubes. I have always been successful." She replied confidently.

"OK, good luck. I hope you have the magic touch." I had that horrible knot in my gut.

After an hour, I went in for my next ten-minute visit to find no feeding tube in Brandon. I found the nurse in charge and asked, "Was she unable to get the feeding tube back in?" She acted as if she didn't know what I was talking about. I explained that the new nurse pulled the feeding tube out because it was clogged, *after* I told her of the horrible procedure Brandon had to go through to have it inserted. I was not happy. I was angry! I didn't want Brandon to have to go through that horrible experience of having a rod shoved down his throat again, on top of having a vent tube in! I let the nurse in charge know that this was totally uncalled for. That nurse was warned not to pull it out.

I went back into my "sanctuary," slammed the door and cried out to God, "It's so unfair. Why does Brandon have to go through all this? He's so helpless, he can't fend for himself. We can't even protect him! Lord it's all up to you. I trust you to protect him."

When I went back for my next ten-minute visit, that nurse was gone. The nurse in charge apologized, and told me that nurse was relieved of her duties and would not be back to care for Brandon, however, he would have to endure the procedure again, and they were very sorry. I stood at Brandon's bedside and cried. I usually went in and stayed positive when I was with him. I would smile at him, tell him it was going to be OK and tell him I loved him. I never let myself cry until after I left his side. I had to stay strong. But my heart just broke thinking of all his poor body had been through over the last two weeks. It's the most excruciating pain for a mother to not be able to make her child all better. A kiss and a band aid would not fix this boo-boo. It was like labor pains. I was actually feeling pain in the abdomen like I was going to give birth again. Only this was much worse, because my heart was breaking too. I would kiss him good-bye, tell him I'd see him in fifty minutes and walk out. As soon as I hit the door the tears would flow, the sobs would wrack, and I'd go to my "sanctuary" until I couldn't cry or pray anymore.

I went to bed that night, closed my eyes and went into that half-awake dreaming stage. I pictured myself in the pitch dark night getting on a roller coaster and already seated in the car was the Lord Jesus Christ inviting me to sit beside Him. He gently placed his arm around me, and put His hand on my shoulder. I could feel the warmth and the gentle pressure of His hand on my shoulder, as if to tell me, "I am on this ride with you, and I will not leave you." I slept.

And up: My *Mom's In Touch* group would come to the ICU and have their weekly prayer time with me. It was such a "thirst quenching" time for me. There is nothing greater in the world than having a group of mothers, all in agreement, pouring their hearts out in prayer for you. It was such an encouragement and I pray God blessed those ladies for their faithfulness.

And down: Brandon developed a severe infection in his lungs that required some very potent antibiotics. They put him in a rotating bed to help get rid of the fluid in his lungs. He also had to routinely have his lungs suctioned out. Brandon craved having this done. He was always requesting to be suctioned. His throat was very sore from all the things being shoved down it and he would also request a numbing spray that they used on his throat as well as pink, minty "sponge suckers" filled with water. I hated seeing him so uncomfortable, but was grateful that he was so awake.

And right turn: Pat returned for another visit to give us some very good news. They would be sending Brandon to one of the top rehab hospitals in the country. There, he would be very well cared for and rehabbed to a point where he could be totally independent. A nurse/case manager would be there in less than a week to evaluate him and see if he was stable enough to travel. This was wonderful news! He could live an independent life and make a good life for himself! I couldn't grasp it. How? How would that be possible? But the hope that soared inside removed all doubt. The Lord would make a way. And maybe He would even recover completely? We still had a two-year window! Pat shared with me as I am writing this, that she was a little bit hesitant about asking permission to send him there. But after seeing the dire situation, there was nothing else but to do the best they could.

And up: Some friends from the Home School group, Leon and Susan, came across an article about a girl who had been paralyzed in an accident and she was given an experimental drug called Sygen. She regained most of her sensation and mobility. We were so excited to hear of such a drug. We spoke to the doctor about it and he said, "Yes, it is still in the testing stage, so we won't know if we are given the drug or the placebo. And since it is still being tested, we don't know if there are any harmful or permanent side effects. There is also a time window. The drug needs to be administered within two weeks after the injury." We were right at two weeks. It would be taking a chance, but what other option did we have? We took the print out with all the information about the drug with us, read it over carefully and decided it was worth a try. Anything was better than nothing! So the doctor put the order in to have it delivered. How blessed we were to have friends doing research for us!

And down: They felt Brandon needed to be removed from the ventilator to see if he was able to breathe on his own. He was still so weak he just didn't have the strength. He code blued again, and they had to reintubate him. His poor throat was scratched again. I went to my sanctuary and I cried out to God again, "Please Lord, don't take my son. I'm not ready to let him go. You have to help him. I don't believe you saved him to let him die now. Not now."

It was beginning to feel like this was never going to end. The crowds of visitors had thinned out considerably over the weeks, now the waiting room was nearly empty. A friend named Jill would always find the time to come and sit with me a while. It was so good to have her there! Those quiet days were when the reality of "life as we knew it" was forever gone. With all the visitors gone, it was a powerful notification that we would be on our own living this nightmare. Nothing would ever be the same. I was starting to lose hope and becoming discouraged. Would Brandon survive ICU long enough to make it to the rehab hospital? How many more code blues could he survive? The aloneness drove me closer to the Lord, which is the best place that I could be.

Just Breathe

I WAS CALLING my parents daily to give them updates on Brandon's condition. They live in the same state that the rehab hospital is located in. They had just left our house, after a two-week visit, the Monday before the accident. I didn't expect them to turn around and drive back right away, as they are seniors and the stress could be overbearing. They were making plans to come back when I found out that we would be staying in the rehab hospital for at least three months. So we decided that they should just wait until our arrival there, since there really wasn't anything they could do here anyway. We were all anxiously waiting to hear when we would be leaving for the rehab hospital.

Several days after the last attempt to remove the ventilator they decided they needed to try it again. Brandon would not be able to be transferred to the rehab hospital until he jumped that hurdle. His lung infection was gone, feeding tube was in and chest tubes were removed. For as critical as he still was, he was stable. They had moved him to the end of the hall, further from the nurses' station, but had a critical care nurse in there with him continuously to monitor his progress. I really liked her. You can tell when you have the right nurse caring for your loved one.

At the start it felt good to see Brandon partially sitting up in his bed with no ventilator! He could actually say hi to us when we came in. It was more of a whisper; you could tell that it was difficult for him to breathe. Chris and I tried to make light conversation, to tell him of other things that were going on outside of the ICU and to try to bring some cheer and encouragement to him. I think we did get him to smile once. He had lived through so much. He would nod or shake his head in response, because it was just too exhausting for him to try to speak.

As time went by we could see he was getting tired. It became increasingly difficult for him to inhale. Chris and I began coaching him, telling him to relax and to take deeper breaths. All three of us were actually breathing in unison. If we could just get a good rhythm going maybe his body would remember how to do it. Crazy thought, I know, but I was desperate. The nurse sat at her table and wrote things down. She checked his oxygen saturation levels, pulse and blood pressure often. I began to get worried for him. His skin color was changing and he was really struggling. His whole body would heave and drop with every breath. It was horrible to watch. No one should have to sit and watch their child fight for every breath. The clock said it was almost 1 a.m. We had been doing this for hours! I could not believe that much time had passed. I asked the nurse, "Is he going to be able to do this all night?" She quietly shook her head. "No, I think you should go and try to get some sleep, and if anything changes I will call you right away." I knew that meant they were going to reintubate him again—a third time. It was the Mother's Knot in the gut that told me so.

We quietly and gently kissed his forehead, told him we loved him and turned for the door. After watching him fight for every breath for the last several hours, I really thought this might be the last time I saw him, the last time I kissed him.

Before I was out the door I was crying uncontrollably. I got to my sanctuary and just cried until I was empty. I was already so breathless from "helping" Brandon breathe that my chest hurt. I couldn't stop the pain. Was it physical? Or was it emotional? It all became one.

I was at the point of surrender. "Lord, what do you want from us? Why are you letting him suffer like this? I have no strength left within me. I have nothing more to ask of you." I began to calm down. The tears were still coming hard but I was more relaxed, limp actually, from sheer exhaustion. I was sitting on the commode, my head resting against the cold wall, when the most painful and difficult thing came out of my mouth, "Lord, if You want him, I give him back to You. I thank you Lord for lending him to me, and for allowing me to be his mom. He is the best son any mother could ask for, but I know, he was Your's first. I cannot bear to see him suffer like this any longer." My heart shattered into a million pieces, yet, I felt that warm hand on my shoulder, the one that I felt on that half-awake -dreaming –roller coaster ride. I had a peace, a peace that passed all understanding. I knew the Lord loved me, and I knew He loved Brandon. There wasn't a safer, more peaceful place Brandon could be than in the arms of Jesus. I almost fell asleep on that commode in that stall. I had so much peace.

When the tears subsided, I gathered what strength I could find and made my way to the waiting room to meet Chris. He held me up as we walked back to the hotel. My whole body, mind, spirit, and soul were completely exhausted.

We cried at the thought of what Brandon had to struggle through as we walked through the night, and we mourned the thought of losing him.

As soon as we got to the room the phone was ringing. I looked at Chris, "They put him back on the ventilator."

"Hello, this is Gail. As soon as you left, we reintubated him. He is resting easily now, so you should too. I will take good care of him, don't you worry," reassured the nurse.

I hung up the phone, and we got on our knees and thanked the Lord for letting Brandon have help again with breathing. I dropped out of my clothes and into bed. As I lay there, I began breathing in the rhythm we had with Brandon. I began to notice how difficult it is to breathe when you concentrate on it and really think about it. Breathing is such a natural reflex it takes no thought. I prayed that Brandon would fall into that natural pattern once he didn't have a machine doing it for him. We so easily take for granted every breath, when it so easily could be taken from us. Every inhale, I would thank God. Every exhale, I would thank God. I asked Him to forgive me for every breath that I took for granted my whole life.

The next morning I walked over to the hospital with a different outlook on this whole situation. Brandon was now God's. I gave him to *Him*. What ever happened now was God's will.

The lady from the rehab hospital arrived and Pat was with her also to tell us that they would be taking Brandon in two days to the rehab hospital. I told her of our long night with Brandon without the ventilator and she told me, "Tell your doctor *not* to remove that ventilator. He can fly out there with it and we will wean him off gradually once he gets out there. We do things a lot differently there than they do it here. It's much easier on the patient." Those were the best words I'd heard in three very long weeks. Pat was mortified to hear of all that he had been through. And she was confident that things would be much better as soon as we were out of there and at rehab.

I looked at Brandon and smiled. We would be out of there soon! I was so anxious to get him into the rehab hospital. I just knew it would get better. It had to be.

Flight to Hope

EXCITEMENT and anxiety were the emotions driving me the next two days. I had to go home and pack for Brandon and myself for a three-month stay at the rehab hospital. I hadn't been home since the accident happened three weeks before. I was somewhat apprehensive to leave the ICU, but I had to pull myself together and get packed.

When we arrived in our town and crossed the 12th Street Bridge my eyes were immediately drawn to the river embankment that so drastically changed everything. I tried to picture in my mind how it all happened. It made my stomach hurt. I never realized how high that embankment was before and would've never guessed the creek was so shallow.

Soon we were in our driveway. There sat Brandon's pickup with its home made wooden bed. It would never have Brandon behind its steering wheel again. That thought brought a tear to my eye. As we walked into the house it was as if we were walking into a stranger's house. It didn't feel at all like home. Everything looked exactly the same as I'd left it. I could envision Brandon running up the stairs three at a time like he used to and Renelle walking down the hall to greet me with a, "Hi, Momma." But it was silent. Haunting. I went to the basement first, to Brandon's room. His bed was still unmade just like he'd left it. Through tears I began to go through his dresser and his closet trying to think of what he might wear or what he might need. It was really hard to imagine him up out of bed and dressed at all! I began packing whatever I could remember that were his favorites.

Then in my suitcase I threw together a week's worth of outfits that I could mix and match that were the most comfortable, along with a couple of pairs of shoes. I hadn't looked through my closet or drawers for three weeks. Chris had been bringing me clothes and taking them back for Mom to wash. It was like everything was new again. I grabbed all the toiletries I thought I might use and a couple of jackets and I was packed and ready to go.

I was so grieved to leave our home—to leave our life, because I knew it would never be the same. I didn't know what the future held but the memories of how it was, would be just that, memories.

We got back in the car and drove back to the hospital. I don't think we were at the house an hour and I was anxious to get back to the hospital. We tried to make a plan of how Chris was going to come and see us but that was impossible. How could we afford it? He just said he would come as often as he could. I grieved more at the thought of doing this without my husband. He had to work, there was no way around it.

The next morning we rose early and headed to the ICU. Brandon was bundled and on the stretcher ready to head for the airport. We would be flying in an EagleMed jet to start our journey to rehabilitation. They loaded Brandon, Chris and I into the ambulance and drove us to an airstrip. There, a small jet was sitting on the tarmac waiting for us. Brandon was loaded in first and once he was all settled with his ventilator and IVs, they seated us. (When the doctor knew that Brandon could go to the rehab hospital with the ventilator they did a tracheotomy for his ventilator tube, so it was no longer in his mouth. It was much more comfortable for him and it would be easier to wean him at rehab.) He could mouth words and I got fairly good at reading his lips.

Chris told the pilots that he and Brandon have always had a fascination with flying. It was a dream for both of them to fly a plane one day. So the pilot told Chris, "Well, why don't you come up here in the co-pilot's seat and fly with me today." Brandon was jealous. The flight nurse said, "Don't you worry, we'll be sending you on a flight of your own with this morphine I'm putting in your IV. This will

That's me getting seated inside and Chris is outside waiting his turn. Brandon was already tucked in.

[47]

guarantee that you have a relaxing and enjoyable flight yourself." Brandon smiled and nodded.

Chris got to wear the headset and even fly the plane! He was like a little boy again, enjoying every minute of it. And Brandon was enjoying his "flight" too.

The unknown was becoming more and more ominous. Would there be more code blues? More surgeries? Would Brandon regain feeling or movement in his body? What did this strange place have in store for us? I was going to miss my family, friends, my support group. I'd be on my own carrying Brandon through this.

We landed at an isolated airstrip and there was an ambulance waiting for our arrival. They made the transfer very quickly and we were off to the hospital. I was so anxious for a new change. Anything had to be better than what we just came through.

When we arrived at the hospital, I couldn't get over how big the place was. Were all these buildings all one hospital? The rehab hospital was connected to another very large hospital that specialized in trauma, so the complex was several blocks in size. They led us to Brandon's room and said someone would be there to transfer him to a hospital bed shortly.

The room was huge in comparison to the ICU cubicle that he was in. It had a very large window. Actually the whole east side of his room was a window! It was beautiful to be able to see outdoors and to be able to watch the sunrise! Brandon hadn't seen the outdoors for three and a half weeks! There were two beds in the room, with a folding curtain to divide the room. No roommate yet, so we had it all to ourselves—two bathrooms, one with a roll-in shower, and closets and drawers on each side. It felt welcoming, and that was a wonderful relief. It was such a stark contrast to

ICU. There it was dark, no windows that I can recall, and the mood was dismal and serious.

Soon two aides were there and introduced themselves. They were very friendly and cheerful. They said, "We heard you've had quite a rough time of it."

Brandon nodded.

"Well, it's going to get a whole lot better now." They transferred him to the hospital cot.

"We are going to take him down for some tests, just because we do things so much differently here than a regular hospital does. We need to evaluate everything for ourselves to determine the best path forward. You can just stay here and relax a bit and we'll be back with him later."

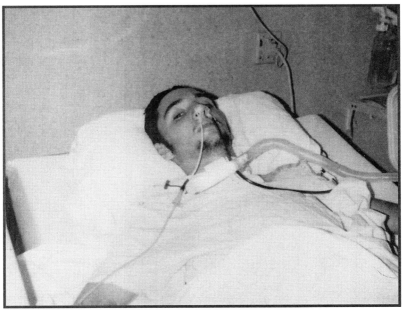

This is a photo the rehab hospital took upon his arrival.

They sounded so positive. My heart was cheered. I could feel relief and confidence returning to my soul. Brandon was going to be OK. This was a good place for him to be.

A short while later a lady arrived to tell me that I would be staying in the apartments right next door to the hospital. Brandon was still gone, so she took us on a brief tour of our immediate section of the hospital. She showed us where the important places were, like the restrooms, cafeteria, and coffee shop. Then down the elevator to the main floor, where right outside the door was a community garden with some paths and benches. It was beautiful! I wanted to sit right down and soak up the sunshine. She led us on to the building right across the yard. That was my new place up on the third floor—the same floor that Brandon was on in the hospital. It was a nice and clean place with a hide-a-bed couch and coffee table in the living room, a fully furnished kitchenette, full bathroom and bedroom. It was comfortable. And right outside my bedroom window, if I craned my head to the far-right, I could see Brandon's window. It was perfect. She handed me the keys and told me where the important phone numbers were listed and wished us all the best.

We didn't take the time to unpack anything. We just left it all sitting inside the door and headed back to the hospital. We took our time walking through the garden and had no trouble retracing our steps back to Brandon's room. It was so quiet and peaceful and the view was wonderful. Peace was taking hold.

A little later they returned with Brandon. I had to ask, "Is he going to be OK?" I had to know if I should prepare for yet another code blue or not.

"He's got a ways to go, but I think he'll recover quickly." She said.

We watched as they transferred him into his bed and hooked up all his necessary tubes. It was the first time I had seen his limp body since the accident. He was so thin. They chatted and laughed and carried on like normal. Normal? Normal! The word bounced around inside my head. Is that what we had been missing? Could we find it again? His aides were busy re-introducing us to it, and it was wonderful. They were telling Brandon that he better get prepared because there wasn't going to be anymore laying around in bed. He was going to have several drill sergeants in his face on a daily basis training him to win this battle. Brandon looked surprised and less than enthused. My heart did a hopeful flutter.

Enrollment and Introductions

WE AWOKE later than usual the next morning, sleeping in felt good for a change. We got dressed and went to the hospital. It was bustling about with patients in wheelchairs, nurses, doctors, therapists, and family members. For the first time I knew that we weren't the only ones being faced with a new and difficult change in our lives. It was encouraging to have others standing alongside of us in this battle. This rehab hospital specialized in not only spinal cord injuries, but traumatic brain injuries as well. It only took a very few minutes to be humbly grateful that Brandon had no brain injuries. My heart went out to those families who had to get to know their loved ones all over again. And I thanked God for protecting Brandon's brain. He could've drown and been deprived of oxygen before the EMS got there. Or he could've hit his head on a rock and caused brain damage.

When we got to Brandon's room, his aide was in there introducing himself and telling Brandon all about rehab and what to expect. Kenny was such a God-send! He was a big teddy bear! He laughed easily and encouraged Brandon on days he didn't want to get out of bed. He showed me where I could do our laundry, where the nurses' station was, and if we ever needed anything, they would be right there. He would also bring me a meal when he brought in food for Brandon. He was so thoughtful and genuinely caring.

Next we got to meet one of his nurses. She was a tiny little thing, and very busy. She would tell us that Brandon had a very large skin wound on his right shoulder blade that he acquired while in ICU. It was as deep as two quarters stacked together and as large as a small chicken thigh (that's what the shape reminded me of). It would take a transcutaneous electrical nerve stimulation (TENS) unit and all three months we were there to heal it up. She also told us that Brandon weighed 120 pounds!

"What? He did weigh 180! You mean he's lost 60 pounds in three and a half weeks?" I asked in disbelief. How could he lose so much weight so quickly?"

"Yes. We are going to have to get right on that and put some weight back on him. We'll have to get the NG tube (the tube pulling the blood out of his stomach) out first, and see if he is able to swallow and then we'll get him started on protein shakes to see if we can get his weight up." She went on to explain, "Spinal cord injury is the second most traumatic injury a body can survive. Being burned over a large percentage of your body is number one. When the injury happens, the metabolism goes into high gear trying to repair everything that's broken, and that requires thousands of calories a day. His metabolism will stay high for several years trying to heal the body, so good nutrition is going to be very important for him. And I'm sure being without the feeding tube for two weeks didn't help. That's a long time to go without any form of nutrition."

Next to appear in the door was the respiratory specialist. He listened to Brandon's chest and explained to him that they would not be removing the ventilator any time soon. He felt compassion that Brandon had so many reintubations and told him that they would be weaning him gradually. A special canula would be attached to his tube that could be capped off from the ventilator. They would start out at thirty minutes the first day, or what he could tolerate, and increase the time a little each day until he was off of it completely. He also explained to us that because of his paralysis, his rib cage would no longer expand and contract with each breath, limiting his oxygen intake. Therefore he would be doing most of his breathing with his diaphragm. They would put on a binder, which looks like a wide elastic band, around his abdomen to support his diaphragm. He was totally confident that Brandon would not be ventilator dependent. People with high neck injuries, at about C-4 and higher, usually are ventilator dependent. I was so thankful to hear him say that he would be free from that breathing machine—one less obstacle to independence.

Following the respiratory specialist was the respiratory therapist. He was a young man, not too long out of school and he was fun! He always had a joke or a silly story to tell. While he was giving Brandon a breathing treatment he said that he'd heard how many times Brandon coded and had to be reintubated. He then told us a story about when he was in medical school learning how to intubate. A classmate and he decided that it would be very educational for them if they intubated each other, completely awake, without any sedation. He said it was so painful it was like swallowing a garden hose. And then, to have it pulled out was a thousand times worse. He said it was the most excruciating pain he had ever felt. It was a decision they regretted, but they did not regret the lesson they learned. They make sure to be as gentle as possible when intubating someone. Brandon shook his head in disbelief. He told Brandon to be thankful for the good drugs that numbed him and erased his memory. Then he asked him if his throat was sore, Brandon nodded. He told him that they would do some checking to make sure that his esophagus was not damaged in anyway. Relief was filling every crack in my heart. Just to listen to their expertise and to hear such encouraging words brought so much peace.

Next was the physical therapist. She did several stretching exercises on his legs and arms and Brandon winced in pain. He had huge knots under his shoulder blades and across his shoulders. The therapist worked to rub those out and said that would be an ongoing problem for a while, just because he's been lying flat on his back for so long after he was used to being active. She showed me how to do it also. It almost seemed like torture to press on those hard knots until they released. I felt sorry for the pain it caused Brandon. Before she left, she gave him a schedule for his daily routine and told him she'd see him in the therapy room soon. It almost felt like he was going to school, with classes and instructors. It was like he wasn't in serious condition at all. They just moved him forward in spite of his condition.

We had a short break before the neurologist came in. He was a man of few words. Very serious, yet very attentive. He asked if we understood what Brandon's injury meant, and if we had any questions.

"Yes, we had requested back in ICU to try the Sygen, but we hadn't received it before we left," I said.

"It is on its way here, and as soon as we get it, we'll hook him up," he said.

"Have you given it here before?" I asked.

He nodded, "We have not been able to see any miraculous results here. But it's worth the try. You are aware that you have missed the two week time frame for the best results aren't you?"

"Yes, we are. But we have to try something, anything. Prayer has been our only other option." I said, trying to muster more faith.

"Prayer is the best option. He created the spinal cord, He knows how to fix it," he replied.

My heart soared to know that Brandon had a believing doctor. This was good!

He went on to explain, "When the spinal cord is bruised, those bruised cells begin to die. Then something unusual to the rest of the body happens. These 'scavenger' cells come along and eat those dead cells and clean the bruised spot up. When this happens it leaves a hollow hole in the cord and then there's no hope for a 'reconnection' to take place. The Sygen is supposed to stop or slow down the dying of the cells and also slow down or disable the scavengers. The spinal cord is the only organ this takes place in—one of the great mysteries of the spinal cord. Sygen worked for the NY Jets football player that was paralyzed on the field, or so they give credit to that anyway."

I could tell we had a lot to learn. They offered classes everyday on spinal cord injury (SCI) or traumatic brain injury (TBI), and we would learn as much as we could in our three month stay. I quietly told the Lord, "If you choose to heal him, I believe this doctor would give you all the credit." As if the Lord needed my suggestions.

Brandon was getting tired. It was so nice to be able to be with him and not have to leave. The weekend was almost here and they didn't have any classes or therapy on the weekends, just outings. Every weekend they offered some kind of outing for the patients and their families to be a part of. I was anxious for us to be able to do that. They held church services on Sundays in one of the conference rooms and several different churches in the area took turns doing the service.

In came the occupational therapist. She would teach Brandon how to feed himself again, brush his teeth, wash his face and use a track ball mouse for his computer. They would show him creative ways to do things to be as independent as he possibly could. I could tell that Brandon was discouraged. He didn't want to have to learn how to do all that again with his limited mobility. She let him know that they were going to wait until his tolerance with being up in a wheelchair was better. However, there were a few things he could do in bed.

Evening was already here when his night aide came in and introduced herself. She was a very sweet and caring girl. She asked Brandon if he'd like a shower. This was going to be a very difficult hurdle for Brandon to get over. We are a very modest family and getting naked in front of a young lady was totally embarrassing to think about, let alone do! I can remember when Brandon was little, I was running his bath water, getting out a clean towel for him, and I turned around to gather his dirty clothes and he was standing there with his hands on his hips, still in his Scooby-Doo briefs, looking at me and said in his little boy voice, "You can get out now."

"What?" I said, not believing my ears.

"Get out," this little man says.

I gathered his dirty clothes while looking in his little eyes, and slowly backed out the door.

"Do you want me to shut this?" I asked, holding the door knob. Up to this point the door remained open at bath time.

He stepped over and closed it himself. I stood on the other side of the door for a moment and thought to myself, my little boy is growing up. Sadly, I threw the dirty clothes in the hamper and went on my way.

That was the last time I ever saw my son undressed and he was probably three or four at the time. As a family we never ran around in front of each other without clothes on.

My little man.

So Brandon was not too sure how this was going to work.

The aide reassured him that he didn't have anything new that she hadn't already seen and that she would cover him with a towel to save his embarrassment. He reluctantly agreed. So while they were showering, Chris and I went to the cafeteria for supper.

The cafeteria was a lot like a school lunch room. It was located in one of the therapy rooms and during a meal time they would set up tables and chairs for the able-bodied to sit at. There were mats and exercise tables and Hoyer lifts and other therapy equipment all around the perimeter, much of which I had no idea what it was used for. We went through the line picking out what we wanted to eat and seated ourselves. The food was surprisingly good! Much better than the usual hospital food. It was so nice to sit and eat together knowing that Brandon was OK and moving into normalcy. Well, a *new* normalcy.

When we got back to the room Brandon was already back in bed and shiny clean. His aide said it took awhile to scrub the mud out of his hair and his ears after three weeks of setting in there. He looked so much better, but I think he was still somewhat uncomfortable, and would have preferred a male aide. I wish he could have talked at this point. We would've had no doubt about how he felt.

The weekend was here and we would have two days to acquaint ourselves with our new surroundings. The hallways were much quieter, therapy rooms were empty, and it was so peaceful for such a large place. We would soon find out that after five days of classes and therapy the quiet weekends would be greatly appreciated. We would spend this first weekend watching Brandon sleep and reflecting on the horrendous roller coaster ride we had just gotten off of, and looking forward to what rehab was going to accomplish. Brandon seemed to be resting much more comfortably, and because of that, we did too.

All of the information and introductions were overwhelming. But it felt so good to be in a positive and hopeful place. Most of the time I felt as if I was floating around on a cloud watching all that was going on around me, yet not a part of any of the activity. It was relaxing and restful for me.

My daily routine became very normal. I would read my devotions early in the morning and go for a walk around the entire medical complex, which was down a long hill and then back up. I lost several pounds doing this excellent work out each day. It was my quiet time, just me and the Lord. On rainy days I would walk inside the hallways of the hospital. There were many miles of those it seemed. I would chat with my neighbors and our roommates and hall mates. Everyone's story was so different from ours, yet so much alike.

I knew the Lord was there. I knew that He was caring for us, that He was providing a way for us. My devotional that first full day was the verse, Jeremiah 29:11: "I know the plans I have for you," declares the Lord, "Plans to prosper you and not to harm you, plans to give you a hope and a future." This became the promise that we would cling to. We knew the Lord loved us and wasn't punishing us for our sins.

He Finally Speaks

IT WAS MONDAY, and Chris had to leave to go back to work. We walked over to the hospital early in the morning so he could say goodbye to Brandon. He would call a taxi to take him to the airport, and when he landed, Mom would pick him up and take him home. It was so hard to see him leave. I worried about how he'd get fed, have clean clothes to wear, and if he'd be lonely. I knew he could do it all for himself, but I was used to doing it for him and enjoyed doing it. I kissed him good-bye and cried when he left. As I watched him get in the taxi and ride away, loneliness gripped me. Suddenly, I could feel that warm, gentle pressure on my shoulder. I knew I was not alone.

On one of the trips Mom made to the airport to pick Chris up, she was sharing the story that her son was on his way home from the rehab hospital from seeing his son, and one of the ladies, also waiting said, "I know who you are talking about! I'm the lady that was sitting in the McDonalds drive thru that day! How is your grandson doing? Our church prays for him every week!" It is so intriguing how interwoven our lives really are. What's that saying, eight degrees of separation? So amazing.

One of the most difficult things about rehab was being separated as a family. We had never been separated before. Renelle would come home when Grandma would come back for the weekend, and then she'd either go back home with Grandma, or stay with friends. She was here and there and everywhere, or so it seemed from hundreds of miles away. Then she would come out with Chris, and stay a week or two with me, and return either with someone who'd come to visit, or with Chris on his next trip out. We would be happily surprised every once in a while with a visit from friends who could make the trip out. It was always so good to see them. It was a glimpse at "normal," but the time always went too fast. I always looked forward to having Renelle come and stay a while. I missed her terribly. She was growing up so quickly in the midst of all this tragedy and I felt as though I wasn't there when she needed me. If I could've been in two places at once, it was at that particular time in our life.

It was so nice that Chris' boss, at the time, would let him work long hours to build them up, and then let him take four and five day weekends to come out to see us. I asked Chris how we were able to afford all the flights. He reminded me of the night of Renelle's eighth grade graduation, when all those people stuffed his suit full of money. And they also had set up a fund at our local bank to help with expenses. That money bought every ticket, and then some, for our entire stay at rehab.

When I arrived back at the hospital, Brandon was being dressed and it felt so good to see him in clothes for the first time in nearly a month. He would be getting into a manual chair that was equipped to handle his portable ventilator, and could also recline to a completely flat position. It was time for my first lesson on how to care for my son.

They told me to put on a pair of gloves and taught me the importance of being as sterile as possible when dealing with his ventilator and all that went with it, to prevent infection. First of all, I had to learn how to suction the mucus out of his lungs. I was petrified! "You're going to trust me to do this?" I asked shakily.

"It's not hard at all. Every caregiver has to learn this. You'll do fine," the nurse encouraged.

Brandon gave me that doubtful look. "OK, I'll do my best," I replied, unsure of myself.

She demonstrated how to sterilely apply the long skinny hose to the vacuum tank, turn the vacuum pump on, insert the hose into the vent and start sucking away, making sure to scrape all sides and the bottom thoroughly. It made me a little woozy listening to the liquid being slurped up, but I knew this was too important to worry about my feelings. Then she handed it to me. "Now you do it," she said easily. Brandon still had that doubtful look on his face, but I did it. And I did it right the first time. Brandon looked relieved. (He always likes to give me a hard time, and tease me). He still enjoyed being suctioned out; it felt good to have that stuff removed that he couldn't cough up.

Next they brought out an ambu bag. I had never seen one before up close, let alone know how to use one. She explained that I was to use this if Brandon went into respiratory distress. She demonstrated how to use it, and then asked me if I had any questions.

"How often will I have to use this?" I asked, a bit unnerved.

"It's very rare that it has to be used at all. But when you

are out and about with him, you'll have to be prepared for anything. There will always be help nearby if something should happen, but let's hope it doesn't," she said.

I was like a nervous new mom, remembering when I brought my new born baby home from the hospital for the very first time and hoped I didn't screw anything up and jeopardize the health and safety of my child.

Then they transferred him into the chair. It was wonderful to see him sitting upright. We began a tour of the hospital therapy rooms. Brandon would get light headed very easily because his blood pressure would drop and we'd have to stop and recline him for a few minutes before going on. It would take a while for him to be upright for any long length of time. I could tell that he was less than interested in the therapy rooms and he was as white as a sheet.

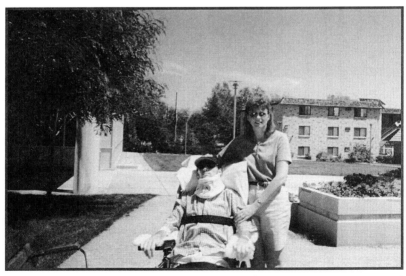

One of our first trips outdoors to the garden.

After the tour, they let us be on our own. I asked Brandon if he'd like to go outside and see the garden area.

It was a beautiful sunny day and he hadn't seen the sun in weeks. As we sat there taking in all the fresh air, I could hear his chest rattling. So I got out the gloves, my hands wouldn't stop shaking, and went through all the steps to suction him out. I did it, no problem! I was so impressed with myself and Brandon half-grinned and shook his head at my pride. I was so confident I told myself I would teach Chris how to do this the next time he came out.

I couldn't wait for the day to come when he'd get that ventilator off so I could hear what he was thinking. I often wondered if he remembered the accident. Did he have nightmares about it? Or would he suffer PTSD from it? I had so many questions for him.

After a week of weaning, he could go nearly all day without the vent. Only at night would they put him back on it, mainly so he'd get a good night's rest. I became a pro at the suctioning, and so far, we never needed the ambu bag.

After the second week came the test. Could he do it a full twenty-four hours? I woke early that morning to get to the hospital, before the aides even made it in. What a wonderful sight to see when I walked in. Still no ventilator! The nurse told me that his respirations remained normal all night and he only had oxygen to help keep his oxygen saturation levels up. That would be the next step, taking him off the oxygen too. It was so much easier for him to be weaned this way, and if he struggled, all they had to do was turn it back on, no reintubations.

Once he was off everything they decided to remove the tube completely. They took him to surgery, removed the vent tube and stitched him back up. His scar is very noticeable. They had never seen a trach hole done quite this big. They offered him plastic surgery, but Brandon opted out of that. That scar is a reminder of how hard he fought for every breath.

Now that he was off the ventilator, we couldn't suction the secretions from his lungs, and he still had them. So next, we had to learn what a "quad cough" was. Since Brandon has no muscle use of his body, and limited lung capacity, coughing was very light and unproductive. So we had to help him. This was done by placing the heal of our hand on his diaphragm, he would take a deep breath, and together he would cough, and we would give a hard quick push to his diaphragm. It simulated a normal cough, but it usually took several attempts before it actually produced, and he was able to get it up and spit it out. This was much more difficult and nerve wracking, but eventually, with practice, we became pretty good at it.

Next, they came in to evaluate his swallowing and speaking ability. He still had some difficulty, due to the feeding tube still being down his throat. But it was about the diameter of a couple of pieces of spaghetti, much smaller than the ventilator or the NG tube. The NG tube had been removed some days before. It was so good to not have to look at the nasty black stuff that was being pulled out of his stomach. His ulcers were healing nicely. His voice was very raspy and quiet. I couldn't wait to talk to him. It had been almost six weeks since he spoke.

That night, after they had him all snug in his bed, I pulled my chair up to the side of his bed, I rested my arms on the side of the bed and put chin on my fist so I could see him at eye level and started asking questions. "Have you been dealing with horrible, scary thoughts this whole time?"

"No," he barely whispered.

"Does it hurt your throat to talk?"

"No."

"So you haven't been having nightmares or anything?"

He shook his head, "No, I just feel like a stupid idiot."

"Why?" I felt sorry for him.

"I don't know how to drive a stupid lawn mower? I've mowed for years!"

"Did something happen to the mower to make it stop working right?"

"No, it just slipped. Every way I pulled the levers, the wheels just slipped. It was going toward the creek, and I couldn't stop it, turn it, reverse it, nothing. The wheels had no traction. I feel so stupid."

My heart broke. He had mowed for years, even on a lever controlled mower, just not one that big, or on a river bank, I reminded him.

"Why didn't I just jump in? Why did I have to dive?" He asked, he had tears in his eyes, and so did I.

"Honey, it's just a natural instinct with you, you always dive. And if you wouldn't have dove, at least six feet away, as Vern told me, you could've ended up under that mower. They had to dig it out of several feet of mud. You would've died," I told him. "I had no idea that creek was only two and a half feet deep, did you?"

"No, it looks deeper than that. Maybe because it's so wide, I don't know."

"Did you know you were paralyzed when you were in the water?"

"I knew something wasn't right. I could see my hands just flopping around in front of my face, and I bit my thumb, and I couldn't feel it."

"You bit your thumb?"

"Yeah, hard too. But I couldn't feel it."

"Were you scared you were going to drown?"

"No, not really. I could see this sun beam shining through the water, and I knew I was going to be OK."

"Wow, son, that is amazing!"

"I had peace. Somehow I knew I was going to be OK."

"Do you remember being rescued by Vern?"

"Yeah, I told him to tell my boss I'll pay him for the mower. My boss had just told me the day before that he had just spent a couple thousand dollars getting that mower fixed and how he had just got it out of the shop that day. I feel terrible now that it's on the bottom of Sand Creek. I jumped off of it and tried to hold it back from the ledge. I remember cutting my leg."

"You tried to stop it from going over?"

"Yep."

"Wow! I don't think Superman could've stopped that big, heavy thing."

"Yeah, I just felt so stupid. I had to try everything to save it." I hated seeing him beating himself up.

"Son, it's not your fault. You did the right thing trying to save it. And when you realized you couldn't, you dove far away from it. For that, I am so thankful! You did the very best you could."

Silence ensued. I think we were both trying to picture the whole scene in our minds.

"I don't really remember much after that."

"You don't remember the ambulance ride?"

"No, not really."

"Well, that's good. You've had a very long battle for survival. I'm glad you don't remember all of it."

I had to stand up, lean over and hug my son. I was so proud of the character this young man had. I don't think any of that would've crossed my mind in that situation—especially feeling the obligation to pay for the mower.

I hugged him for a very long time. I only wished he could've hugged me back.

It was late, I wanted to talk so much more, but I didn't want to wear out his voice. We'd talk more tomorrow. I told him I loved him, and I was so glad that he made it out alive.

We said good-night and I headed for the apartment. It was late, but I had to call Chris, like I did every night, and tell him about our conversation. Chris also felt bad for Brandon's feelings, but he too was proud that Brandon handled it all with such character. That was the first night I actually slept with a smile on my face. I thanked the Lord again for saving my son, and being able to communicate with him again. I couldn't wait for his swallow evaluation in the morning, to see if he would get his first taste of food in six long weeks.

When the speech pathologist arrived the next morning, she brought a tray of all sorts of things for Brandon to try. Pudding, jello, yogurt, toast, eggs, a protein shake, and a glass of water. I don't remember the exact order that she fed him these, but he seemed to swallow all of them just fine. Except for the water. He coughed and sputtered and gasped for air. The pathologist then knew that they would have to thicken all of his drinks for a while until he could handle drinking plain liquids. It made things look less appetizing, but it was better than risking another aspiration. She explained that she thought he would eventually get his ability back and that removing the feeding tube, therapy and more healing needed to happen first. We briefly discussed putting the feeding tube in surgically through the abdomen, directly into the intestines, but decided to wait and give Brandon a chance to increase his calorie intake first.

Being able to eat would be such a huge step towards healing. He had been so malnourished for so long, it would be good to see his strength come back and some weight come back on. He was always a big eater. Practically a whole box of cereal would be consumed for breakfast, two or more sandwiches for lunch, and always a second helping for supper. Not to mention snacking during the day. I was anxious to see his voracious appetite return.

Next, the dietician had a long talk with him about the importance of proper nutrition. Since he would be sitting in a chair for the rest of his life, skin sores were going to be his biggest enemies. Good nutrition, good hydration, and frequent weight shifts would be preached and pounded into his head constantly for the next three months. It would be the difference between life and death for a victim of any type of paralysis.

The number of calories required on a daily basis was phenomenal! It was in the thousands! Since his metabolism was working in overdrive, he had to consume lots of calories to keep up. Gaining weight would not be easy, but we definitely needed him to quit losing weight. Protein would be pushed hard, as well as ice cream and anything else that could put on the pounds. Now all he needed was that appetite.

Since he was off the ventilator, the NG tube was gone, no more IVs and his tolerance to being up in a chair was improving, it was time to bring on the therapy!

Basic Training

EVERY FRIDAY, someone would bring by a schedule for the week. There were several therapy sessions, as well as several educational classes. And it was required that Brandon be in attendance to all of these. I went with him the first few weeks to learn as much as I possibly could about his condition. After a couple of weeks he would go to therapy on his own, but I still attended the educational classes. I had to know everything he was going to face. On the days that I didn't go, I would sit in his room or at my apartment and cross-stitch or read.

Many people we knew were prepping for Y2K, remember that? They would ask, "Now, you are stocking up on water and canned food and things you'll need for Brandon aren't you?" I wasn't the least bit interested in stocking up for a manmade disaster. I just said, "Well, I don't really know how to prep with all the new needs we're going to have, so I guess we'll just have to trust the Lord to see us through." He had seen us through so many horrible things already, I doubted He'd walk away from us now. It seemed so ridiculous.

In occupational therapy, they pulled his chair up to this machine where they would strap his hand to these ropes attached to pulleys, and place a wrist brace on with a slot for a spoon or a fork, and they would raise his arm, parallel to the floor and have him try to bring the fork to his mouth. This proved to be a very difficult task at first. He had lost so much muscle mass, not to mention use. He would also have to practice this in bed when they would bring him his meals. I had to help him for a little while, until he gained enough strength to be able to do it himself. He would wear himself out trying to bring the fork to his mouth and would be too tired to eat at first. But with time and strengthening, it wasn't long and he was able to do it himself. Nowadays, he doesn't even need the wrist cuff and hasn't for a long time.

The spinal cord is such an interesting and complex organ. The brain is the power source and the spinal cord is the power strip, where all the nerves are "plugged in." Your level of injury determines where the power strip short circuited. Brandon is a C-5, C-6, C-7 quadriplegic, so his function is short circuited at C-5, the highest level of his injury. So, only his biceps function normally. That is how he is able to do the things that he does. Everything below that has been "short circuited" from the power source.

He was becoming increasingly aggravated at his attempts during therapy and I noticed him watching other patients who had lower levels of injuries accomplishing much more. I think this discouraged him and really frustrated him. I, on the other hand, tended to watch those with higher levels of injuries, and felt encouraged that Brandon was able to do what he was doing. It was a battle that Brandon would have to get the victory over and come to that very hard place of acceptance.

Here is a diagram of the levels and functions of spinal cord injury.

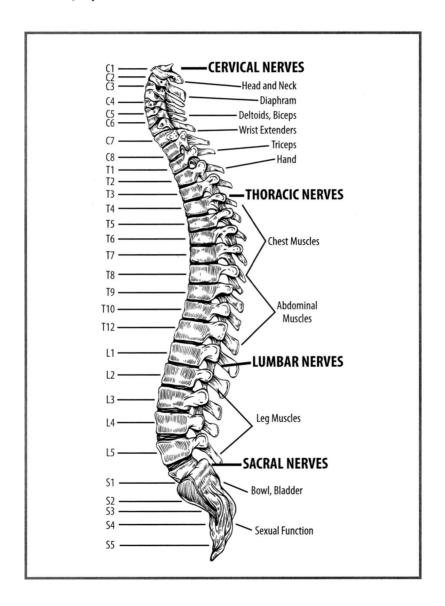

One day in physical therapy, Julie, his therapist, felt a twitch in Brandon's wrist! This is called a wrist flexor and it comes in at the C-6 level. Did the Sygen bring some repair after all? She would make him work it, but not too much, or else he could fatigue it and it wouldn't come back for days or even weeks. We were so excited! Could even more function return? I thanked God and begged him to bring more healing. If he could get full function of the wrist flexor, he would be able to learn to do so much more, including pushing himself in a manual chair, and transferring himself from bed to chair and back again. It would mean a lot for independence! We were so hopeful.

Julie also did a pin pricking test often to see where Brandon had sensation. They had a diagram of the human body and they would color in the areas where he had normal feeling and stripe the areas where he had abnormal feeling. Abnormal feeling is when she would poke him with the pin and he wouldn't feel the pricking, but it would feel more like poking, like with a finger. He could feel it, but it wasn't normal. He has abnormal sensation on the underside of his arms, so when he's sitting out in the hot sun and the arms of his chair become blistering hot, he can rest his arms on the arm rests and not feel the burning. That could be dangerous. There are so many things to think about when sensation isn't normal, that we take for granted.

The human body is so amazing. We are fearfully and wonderfully made. That became more and more obvious as we learned about his injury.

Brandon was making so many great strides in his recovery. Although he really didn't recognize it. To him, he was still paralyzed and unable to move or feel anything. It was becoming more and more difficult to keep him encouraged.

His appetite had increased wonderfully and he was able, on most days, to meet the calorie requirements. The decision was made to pull the feeding tube. Now the only tube he had left was his catheter.

The doctor visited with us about his options concerning this, and we made the decision to have it surgically installed from the outside directly into his bladder. It's called an indwelling, or superpubic catheter. It has been found to cause less bladder infections, and only needs to be changed once a month. I would learn how to replace these also, and Brandon can talk someone through a change if it becomes blocked and one of his caregivers isn't around to change it. They really pounded that into his head too—that he is his own main care giver. He will know his body the best and has to know how to care for it. As a matter of fact, they told him that he will have to tell his doctor, when he gets home, how to treat him. Most doctors do not have a complete understanding of what goes on in a quadriplegic, each injury is somewhat unique, Brandon would have to teach them. Now that was a scary thought. The importance of these classes became very clear. We needed to take them very seriously.

One difficult day, Brandon was feeling really depressed and asked what I thought of assisted suicide. He had realized that even if he wanted to kill himself, he really couldn't do it by himself. This was the last thing I wanted to talk to him about, I didn't want him to even consider such a thing. I told him that I thought he was being very selfish wanting to end his life. What about us? What about his family? How were we supposed to go on and live our lives without him? Didn't he see that he could still make a good and happy life? He informed me that I was the one being selfish, that

I should be willing to let him die so that he wouldn't have to go through this hell of not being able to do anything for himself. I nodded in agreement. Yes, I was being very selfish. I am supposed to die first, not him. I should be able to live out my life being able to see him grow and mature and succeed in life without throwing in the towel and ending it early. I wanted him to find happiness, hope and love. I wanted him to have all the good things in life, to find success and contentment. I knew it was going to be difficult, but with God's help it was possible. He didn't seem convinced. It would take time to accept his new life.

I wanted to be able to just hold my son and comfort him. It's so frustrating, for a mom like me (I rocked my babies until their feet touched the floor) to not be able to hug or hold my child and I imagined that he felt so isolated and "untouchable." So I asked him if I could pull him over to one side of his bed, and crawl in on the other side. He said, "Sure." So I did, and I put my head on his shoulder and held him, and cried with him. I gave him the pep talk and told him that we could do this. "We can make the best of what we have and still find meaning and purpose in our life." I told him we would be there to help him through everything we possibly could. It was so nice to be able to be close to my son.

We were lying there watching TV and in his nurse stepped in the room. She stopped in the doorway and did a double take.

"Are you lying in bed with your son?" she asked.

"Yes, I am," I said, matter of factly. "Is that OK?"

"Well, to be honest with you, you're the first person I've ever seen do this. I think it's a great idea! You just stay right there and I'll work around you."

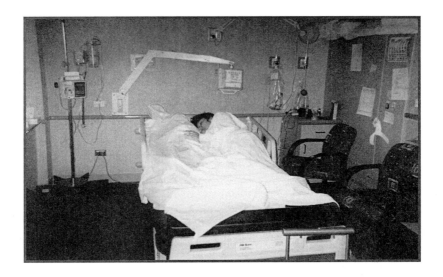

That became the norm in Brandon's room. Chris would lie in bed and talk to him when he came for a visit, Renelle would lie in bed and watch TV, and one time, Renelle, Brandon and I all watched TV in bed together, Brandon in the middle. We didn't have to worry about Brandon wiggling around and pushing us out, we teased him. Three in the bed, two in the bed, the nurses just never knew what they might find! It became a cozy family bed!! Sometimes the nurse would threaten to give all of us a shot, or accidentally give the shot to someone other than Brandon. It was a good time for all of us.

Soon our roommates were doing it too, and the nurse came in one day and said it was becoming contagious, more and more patients were having family members in their beds. I was so happy to think that I may have started an epidemic of this kind. It had to help with healing! Before his accident, I would have never even given this a thought.

The Basic Training was in full swing. Recreational therapy had us going on field trips to the zoo, to this really nice, big mall and sailing. They would actually transfer patients into sail boats and take them around a small lake. Brandon opted to sit on the shore and watch. The water

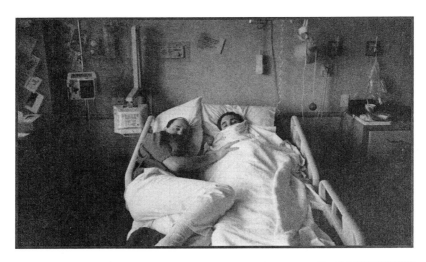

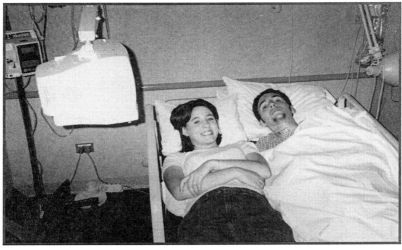

wasn't anything that appealed to him anymore. We had the joy of sharing that day with some friends from the home school group. Brandon played basketball with two of their three sons, Sam and Jed, and their dad, Ron, was the coach. His wife Teresa and their other son Ben were there for the visit also. It was bittersweet. The memories of them playing ball together were difficult, but the present company was wonderful.

Trips to the mall were not enjoyable for Brandon at first. He had a hard time getting used to the stares and being treated like he was mentally retarded. It is amazing to watch people who are unfamiliar with someone being in a wheelchair. They speak louder and slower as if you are hard of hearing or you have low comprehension. Or they are overly helpful. It would be something that Brandon would have to overcome and try teach others how to treat someone who is paralyzed.

Sometimes when I would encourage Brandon to try something new he would say, "I'm handicapped remember?" or "I'm disabled, I can't do that." I would emphatically say, "You are not disabled or handicapped, you are physically challenged!" You can still do so many things, it just won't be as easy to do them. It will take more effort and more determination, but don't ever let yourself be handicapped. You can do anything that you are determined to do. You still have a very fine mind, and lots of creativity. You will just have to find new ways to use these gifts!"

Brandon was trying to enjoy himself, but all he could see was what he was missing, and what he couldn't do. Being seventeen and watching your life plans get blown away is very difficult to overcome. Sometimes these outings were just painful reminders of what he wouldn't get to do. But I had to encourage him to try to find a new enjoyment in it all. Try to look at life with a different set of eyes. Be thankful that you are alive to see the zoo, shop in the mall, or enjoy the view. But it was a battle that only he could win, no one else could do it for him.

My parents would come every weekend and take me grocery shopping and visit with us for the weekend. Sometimes they would go on outings with us too. One weekend Mom brought homemade goulash and we took it up and shared it with Brandon. That was the best I'd seen him eat in a long time. Mom makes excellent goulash and it was one of Brandon's favorite. It seemed to bring some normalcy to life. We all enjoyed dinner together.

We decided after that, we needed a takeout night. Once a week we would pick a local restaurant and call in our order. Sometimes his aides would join us, but not often, as the hospital was usually full of patients. Take out night was a fun and enjoyable move toward normal for us. The Chinese was our favorite, and it was ordered often.

We always looked forward to visitors coming out. Grandma Ruth came with her friends, Pete and Shirley, and they decided I needed to get away. So they took me for a drive into the mountains while Grandma spent time with Brandon. It was a nice little get away, and I enjoyed it very much. But I was ready to get back to see how Brandon's day went, and if anything happened while I was away.

One day in therapy, one of the therapists told me, you really ought to consider going home, and letting Brandon be here by himself. It would give him a chance to be totally independent from his mom. And you could get back to your life. *My life?* I thought, this *is* my life! I looked at Brandon, trying to read his mind, and said,

"We'll have to talk about that. I've never even thought about doing that."

When we left therapy, I was thinking maybe Brandon wants me to go? So I asked him, "Do you want me to go back home and leave you here alone?"

"No way," he said. "I can't imagine that."

I was so relieved. I couldn't even begin to think what it would be like to be several hundred miles away from my child who was in a rehab hospital struggling to make a new life for himself. Not at seventeen, maybe twenty-five, but not seventeen!

However, we had met several people who were in there recovering alone. One young man, I think he was eighteen, had no one. Not one family member or friend with him. My heart went out to him. He was injured when he came home early one morning from partying to find his mom up waiting for him and she was mad. She started yelling at him and he ran up the stairs to his room to get away from her. He ran into his bedroom, slammed his door, did a running jump onto his bed (which was pushed up against the wall with a window) hit the bed and bounced, then flew out the second story window, head first, and broke his neck at the C-2 level when he hit the ground. Ventilator dependant and no one to help or encourage him. He would be living out his days in a nursing home. If I had a desire to adopt anyone, it was him. I felt so sorry for that poor guy.

Stories like that, in a strange kind of way, brought hope. If someone else could survive this and move on with life, so could we.

Brandon's roommate was in his fifties, and a truck driver. One windy day, he was rolling the tarp over his trailer and the wind caught the tarp and pushed him off the ladder.

He landed on his rear end and shattered his L-1 vertebra. He could walk but not without an aide, like a walker or crutches. Most days he would be riding in a chair.

Our first roommate was a semi-pro baseball player, and he was sitting in his mother-in-law's porch swing, gently swaying back and forth when the beam the swing was bolted to broke loose and he crashed to the floor and the beam came down and hit him on the head. Shattered his C-3 vertebra; he would be a ventilator dependent quadriplegic.

When I looked around and heard all of the tragic stories, I found hope. Most of the patients were survivors of car wrecks. Several were injured diving into unknown waters. Twelve thousand people a year survive a spinal cord injury. If all these people can go on with their lives and make the best of them, we can too. For me, that was the most beneficial part of being at the rehab hospital, seeing others go through this and come out OK. For Brandon it was a lot tougher, he had to do the recovering and the therapy, and come to accept his "new" body.

We also got to witness the phenomenon called *the media*. We happened to get to rehab one month after the most gruesome school shooting in our nation's history. Several of the students were at this hospital rehabbing. It was nothing to see a mob of media storming the halls after a class to see if they could catch one of these victims. It was really sad to see them hiding in restrooms or empty offices to avoid the cameras and questioning. Some of them just wanted to be left alone and not be on national television. As they were one by one released to go home, the media began to thin out. Brandon and Renelle accidentally were caught in a picture that was printed in People Magazine. It's of their backside, so no privacy lost.

Brandon had his good days too. I remember one day I came back from the apartment to find him leading a "train" with his nurse, and two or three of his aides around the hallways. The nurse and the aides were sitting in chairs or stools that were on wheels and they latched onto Brandon's chair and to each other and made a train. He would turn the corners as fast as his chair would let him so he could "crack the whip" with his passengers. They were all laughing and giggling and having a grand ole time. People were coming out of their rooms to watch the fun. I always loved seeing glimpses of his old fun self shining through. He can be very ornery and mischievous. It did my heart good to see him having fun, as I know, it did his too.

We received so many cards from people back home. Many from people we didn't even know. Renelle was faithful to email the newspaper at home and give them updates on Brandon's condition. Whenever a new story came out in the paper, the cards came flooding in. It was so overwhelming. We didn't know how to show our gratitude. I would tell Renelle to make sure and have the paper print a "thank you" from us. Their kindness was such an encouragement. I "wallpapered" an entire wall of his room with cards from home, from top to bottom. The nurses even stood in awe. It was a good kind of overwhelming. In some ways it helped to overcome the feeling of being alone.

We spent most of our free time between therapies and classes out in the garden. Brandon loves the sun! Still to this day, on a warm sunny day, that's where you'll find him. We'd sit out there and talk, sleep or just sit quietly and enjoy the view.

Pat came back out to check on our progress and was very impressed with how well Brandon was doing. She let us know that the wheelchair was going to be ordered as soon as they fitted him properly and that we needed to attend the van clinic. This was when the hospital would have several different makes and models of wheelchair accessible vans parked outside in the parking lot so patients could "try them on" to see which would work the best for them. Since Brandon is so tall, (he actually grew another inch that year) he wears a size fourteen shoe and this would prove difficult when trying to get him behind the wheel of a van. His feet would not allow him to pull all the way forward. They could put all kinds of modifications in a van to where it is all hand controlled, making it easier for a quadriplegic to drive. However, it would still be very difficult for Brandon to drive. He decided that it wouldn't be safe for him, or anyone else on the road, to have him behind the wheel of a vehicle. He didn't feel he had the strength or the stamina to be able to drive for any length of time.

Because of his height they would have to lower the floor and raise the roof of a full size van. They would also have to raise the doorway as well, so he wouldn't hit his head coming into it.

There was so much to think about and to plan for. Pat also asked about making modifications to our home. I told her we had a huge back yard, so there was plenty of room for an addition. So it was decided that would be the solution to meet his need for handicap accessibility. An addition that was all handicap accessible, with a totally handicap accessible roll-in shower, large bedroom/office, and a family room. What a blessing that would be! Pat was always way ahead of us on knowing what we were going to need. I had never even given a thought to any of that. I was still too busy learning all I could about his health and thinking about going home that those things hadn't even crossed my mind. She was so wonderful, and took such good care of us.

With all the great strides Brandon was making he still had some tummy trouble. Acid reflux and a decreased appetite were his main complaints. A new intern had come on staff and decided to have Brandon try a brand new drug. They added it to his lunch time pills. By supper time, he was sick. Really sick.

A Very Long Night

WE CAME inside for the evening and Brandon said he didn't feel good. And before we could put him to bed, he was vomiting. His aide got him undressed and put to bed and he was vomiting again. He hadn't eaten much of anything that day, so a food borne illness was not a concern.

The nurse said she'd bring him a ginger ale and thought maybe he had caught some kind of a bug. He took a few sips and rested his head. But before long he was vomiting again. I had that Mother's Knot in my gut that was telling me to ask about the new drug they started him on. Could that be the culprit?

The next time I saw his aide, I asked her, "Could it be the new drug he started taking today?"

"Well, that medication is supposed to help with tummy trouble, so I doubt it's that."

Brandon was vomiting again.

I thought, "Surely this will end soon, he can't have that much in his stomach since he didn't eat anything." Maybe that was is it, maybe he needed to take that medicine with food? So they brought him some crackers to try. Nope, up they came.

I walked out to the nurses' station and asked to see the PDR. I had to read for myself about all the medications he was on and what the side effects were and about mixing them all together. In my research I found that all of them had nausea and vomiting as a side effect. What? Pills that are supposed to help with digestion cause can cause nausea and vomiting? Makes no sense to me. But, I've never been a fan of pharmaceuticals. Now my son was on six or seven of them—three of them for his stomach alone. I again pointed out to the aide that Brandon was fine until he started that new drug.

Brandon was still vomiting, that yellow, vile bile I called it. So they called the doctor to seek his advice. He recommended a shot to stop the vomiting. It was about three hours into his very long night. We turned the lights down low and encouraged him to go to sleep and maybe that would end the retching. This really scared me though. I couldn't leave his side for fear of him aspirating and going through the very same hell that we had just escaped.

But that didn't help, he was vomiting again. The doctor made a special visit to check on him, since it was after hours. He asked him about his day, did he have anything emotionally hard to face that day? Maybe that was what had started it all.

Well, as a matter of fact he did. We had been learning in class about the sexual/reproductive health of a quadriplegic and some very hard things to talk about were discussed. Sex would not be normal and reproduction could happen if he banked his sperm now before the motility was gone. Shortly after a spinal cord injury the sperm lose their swimming ability and a paralyzed person becomes sterile. At seventeen, he really hadn't given much thought to having a family. I mean yeah, it's in the back of his mind to have little ones running around, but he isn't really "planning" it yet.

Which all led to the thought, "What girl would want to marry me? I would just be a burden, and no girl deserves to live like this." That was how he was feeling about it all. Horribly. I have to admit, as his mom and possible future grandma to his children, it tore me up inside too. I couldn't hold back the tears as I slowly erased the picture in my mind of little "Brandons" running amok, causing havoc. That was a dream that I too would have to give up, and it was hard. Brandon was excellent with children and they loved him. He would've been a good dad. And I would've loved those grandbabies.

I tried to reassure him that there would be plenty of women that would fall in love with him. Not girls—it would have to be someone who was mature enough to see life from his perspective. Girls are still vain about a lot of things, it would take a woman who has lived some life and would appreciate his kind heart and his respect for women. Someone who, when they looked at him, didn't even see his chair or his disability. Only his ability to make her happy.

So really, our conversation that day had really been quite a downer. I guess it could be emotional pain causing all this nausea. He was vomiting again. Another shot was given. I was really becoming worried. How could someone vomit this much? They brought in an IV of fluids so that he wouldn't dehydrate, and gave him more stomach medicine—including the new drug.

Every twenty minutes I was holding the pan under his chin, as he wretched his guts out. I am the kind of person that when I see someone puke, I want to puke, so I was feeling extremely ill myself not to mention scared for what was going on with my son. Nothing they tried was working. This went on the entire night. Every twenty minutes.

By sunrise I was exhausted, nauseated and emotionally frazzled. His day time aides came in and gave me a big hug and told me to go to the apartment and get some sleep. They would stay with Brandon. Poor Brandon. He was miserable and no one seemed to know what to do about it.

I went back to the apartment and prayed. I told the Lord that Brandon had been through enough. And to please help his stomach to calm down so he could rest. I was somewhat mad that God was allowing these horrible things to happen. What would it take, what did we have to do to get His favor? What? I slept, but it wasn't a restful sleep.

When I awoke, I dreaded going back over to the hospital to see how things were going. Brandon had stayed in bed all day unable to sleep and was more exhausted than I was. They were encouraging him to eat and drink any way and maybe his stomach would calm down. At least he wasn't vomiting every twenty minutes, but he was still vomiting. I began to think this would never end.

When the nurse came in with his next dose of meds, I asked her if I could refuse the new one. She looked at me surprised. I told her that I just had a sneaking suspicion that Brandon was allergic to it or something, for him to react so violently shortly after taking the first dose. She looked at Brandon and told him that he would have to be the one to refuse it.

"Yeah, let's give it a try, see if it helps to stop the vomiting," he said.

So she removed that pill from his handful. I just hated

that they had him on so many drugs. So when the doctor came in for his daily visit, he asked why we refused it. I said, "Doesn't it just raise a red flag to you? We're supposed to look for adverse side effects when taking a new medication and this, to me, seems like an adverse side effect." I couldn't understand why no one else was seeing this! To me it was obvious! Yes, Brandon had a bad emotional day, but he's had many of those over the past two months. I couldn't believe it was only that.

"Well, I don't think it's in his best interest to take him off of it. We'll be putting it back in to his regimen tomorrow and see how he does," he said.

I felt so helpless and untrusting. Brandon had been doing so well and accomplishing so much and here we were, less than a month from returning home and now this. It was slowing him down, making him weak, and he would be losing weight.

I asked Brandon if the emotional turmoil was more than he could bear. And he reassured me that he didn't think it was that. Yes, all these things are hard to deal with, but he wasn't despondent. Now he was just sick. All the time.

Returning Home

I CAN'T EVEN really put into words the depth of disappointment I felt now that Brandon was so sick. He eventually got to the place where he would go ahead and get out of bed and go to therapy and classes. But he always had to have his barf pan on his lap everywhere he went. I would walk into therapy just to say hi to Julie, his therapist, and she'd be holding the pan under his chin while he puked away. It became the norm. His therapists, nurses, and aides just automatically responded to his moan, get the pan and quickly put it under his chin. What a way to have to live.

He would take a bite or two of his food just to make me happy and the rest of his meal would be wasted. In classes he would have to recline to almost a full lying down position in order to make it through. I just knew it had to be that drug.

When the doctor came in to make his rounds, I again said that I thought it was the new drug that was making Brandon so sick. Of course I don't have years of medical school with big initials behind my name so my Mother's

Knot was dismissed. He did say that he would take him off of one of the other stomach meds to see if that would make a difference. I was happy at least with some small attempt at finding a solution. Then I asked him, "Will he ever be able to be completely off these medications or will he be on these for the rest of his life?" The doctor then told me that as soon as he was home and I was making all the decisions that I could gradually take him off of anything I didn't think he needed. I was ecstatic! That new drug was going to be the first one to go! We only had a couple weeks left and we would be going home.

Removing the one stomach med did seem to help a little bit. Brandon was down to vomiting only once or twice a day now (as if that's a good thing?) and his tolerance for sitting up was getting a little better. I just couldn't get over how much he had to go through! What did the Lord have in mind? There had to be a reason for his struggle to survive. But I had no idea what it was.

Therapy and classes became all about going home. I was ready to go home, but in so many ways it was so frightening. Was I going to be able to care for all of his needs? What if something happened, some kind of emergency? Would I know what to do? Not to mention what was life at home going to be like? We had gotten comfortable at the hospital with the people, the routine, and the way of life. But we would be leaving all of that. We would be completely on our own. It was so scary!

They were teaching me more about his care and when Chris was there, he too was included in these educational sessions. We learned how to transfer Brandon from the bed to the chair using a sliding board. This method is helpful if the people doing the transfer don't have much strength and need the help of a board. It can be hazardous if not done correctly because you can cause a skin sore on his bottom if you "drag" it on the board.

The next method was the two man transfer. One of us would get behind Brandon, the heavy end, so it was usually Chris, and I would get the front end under his knees. We would lean him all the over so his head practically touched his knees, Chris would put his hands under his rear end, count to three and both of us would lift and move him into his chair. This method worked the best for us and we didn't have to worry about the board causing a skin sore. The therapists could do a one man transfer and they made it look so easy, but I didn't even want to attempt it. I didn't want to drop him or hurt him in any way.

They showed us how to change his "super tube," which is what we called the super pubic or indwelling catheter. This was also a very sterile procedure that had to be followed step by step correctly. The first few times I did this, it made me woozy. To be able to look in the hole in his stomach and see urine and know that the tube I'd be reinserting was going directly into his bladder was nerve wracking. Then once it's in, you take a syringe of air and blow up a small balloon that is part way up the tube, but still inside his abdomen, and that is what keeps the tube in. The balloon stops it from falling out. Whoever it was that invented that super tube was a genius!

The next lesson was a little more difficult because it required Brandon having to lose more of his modesty. It was the bowel program. Quadriplegics cannot eliminate their own bowels so someone has to do it for them. He had been having this done by his aides, usually when I wasn't in the room, but now Chris and I had to learn it. Home health aides in our home state are not licensed to do this and we would have to pay a nurse to come in and do it if we didn't learn how to do it ourselves. So they taught us to lay him on his left side because that is the side the bowels empty out of and gravity would help it along on that side. We would place a "blue pad" under him then we would have to insert a suppository and let it "cook." That was the term his aides used for waiting for the suppository to do its job. Most of the time his body would eliminate on his own this way, but then there were also times when we would have to digitally stimulate in order for the waste to move down. We learned the importance of a high fiber diet and preventing constipation as much as possible. Bowel programs become increasingly more difficult when constipation occurs. Brandon also learned the step by step process, so just in case he needed a complete stranger to help him for some reason, he would know how to teach someone.

Recreational therapy would have classes for the patients where they were to just go riding around town to see if there were wheelchair cutouts on the streets for sidewalks and what to do it there wasn't. So many towns, still to this day, do not have accessibility for wheelchairs to be able to cross a street from sidewalk to sidewalk. So then they have to ride in the street to the next driveway to be able to once again get on the sidewalk. This can be very dangerous with the many distracted drivers on our streets today. I had never even given that a thought before. I never needed it, so I never noticed it. That's how it is for most of us.

Then they were to go to the grocery store for an item, any item. Brandon would have to ask a complete stranger to get something off the shelf and place it in his lap because he can't lean over to get it himself. And when he got to the check out he'd have to ask the clerk to reach into his lap, get the item and his wallet and take the money he owed her. This was very hard for Brandon. He did not like having to ask complete strangers to help him. Brandon was always the person offering to help someone else, not the one on the receiving end. Plus, he would have to trust them with his wallet! I was really having my eyes opened to the difficulty he would be facing to be independent. I always had a tendency to do it for him. I was scolded several times by his therapists that he needed to do it for himself. I wasn't always going to be there to do it for him. That was so hard for me! I hated to watch him struggle, almost to the point of tears sometimes. I'm his mom and I wanted to remove any struggle or pain he had. But I knew it wasn't helping him gain his independence. I would have to learn tough love.

We got to sit outside and relax a lot the last week we were there. Our schedule had freed up quite a bit since we first started. It was really kind of a letdown. We had been working so hard to gain strength, weight and knowledge, and now with no other goal in mind to work toward, all we had were thoughts about going home.

We both knew it was not going to be the same. Insurance would hire contractors to start building an addition on to our home. That was exciting, yet hard to imagine. What would it look like? How easy would it be for Brandon to get around? How much room would he have? His bedroom was in the basement with a king size waterbed that he just got when we moved in less than a year ago. He wouldn't be returning to that one or the waterbed. It was more of looking at what had to be given up, erased, instead of looking forward. For some reason looking forward was too foggy. Nothing seemed to become a vision of hope and promise.

I am a daydreamer. I used to watch Brandon playing basketball and my mind would rewind the "memory video" of his life and I could remember him learning how to ride his bike without training wheels, and how determined he was to get it mastered. Then I would fast forward the "video" to see him teaching his own son to ride without training wheels. I did this with both of my children, a lot. I'd fantasize about what they would become and the success and happiness that they would have, and I would try to provide them every opportunity to find happiness and success.

But now the video had become a slide show. Little pictures of the past would come to mind, one at a time, but there was no longer a motion to them. They were still, just a snapshot. And the fast forward no longer worked. It was complete darkness and silence.

Then there was school. Homeschooling would take on a whole new dimension. I no longer had the passion or the drive to even want to do it. Brandon was unable to hold a pen and write anything, it would all have to be re-thought. And Renelle, she still had two years to go. I would have to dig deep to find the will to finish with her. The passion I once had for that was gone.

And what about basketball? It hurt to even think about going to a game to cheer the team on. And Renelle, she was still playing and still wanted to play! And I wanted her to, but somehow it hurt inside. It was like eating a hot fudge sundae in front of someone who couldn't eat sweets and waving it under their nose. Brandon said he didn't mind and that Renelle should play, but it hurt.

Everything about going home hurt. We would be walking back into the past to our old life and renovating it. It would be messy and hard work. And renovating doesn't get done over night. It was going to take time. So many things that we used to have in common with our friends were no longer there. Everything about our lives, about us, had changed dramatically. It would be a chore to once again find common ground. The goals, desires, dreams, and worries that everyone else had, were not at all like ours.

Then there was saying our good-byes. We had grown so close to our medical staff. They were so caring and encouraging. They knew the "new" Coleman family better than anyone else. They lived our horror and our pain with us, bandaged us, rallied us and put us back on the right path. It was going to be very difficult to say good-bye. Would we be OK without them?

So many things were going through our minds. Brandon couldn't imagine what his life would be like either. What would he do all day? Where could he go? Who would want to go with him? It was too much to even try to comprehend. I just said, "We will cross that bridge when we get there." We would do whatever we had to do to make a reasonable, happy life with God's help.

Before we knew it the day had come. It was September 16th, my thirty-fifth birthday, and we were going home. What a wonderful gift! To have our whole family back under the same roof was such a heart-warming thought!

Chris and his brother Keith drove the loaner van out to the hospital. Having it out there would give us some time to practice learning how to load and lock-down then unload Brandon in and out of the van. The reason for the loaner van was because ours was still in the shop getting all of the modifications done to it. It would be ready in a couple more weeks and we would make a trip to switch them around.

We packed all of our bags, Brandon's new power chair, and some medical equipment and loaded them into the van, then started saying our good-byes. It was a tearful event. Good tears, but heart wrenching just the same. They not only cared for Brandon, they cared for our whole family.

It was decided a week or two before dismissal that it would be best for Brandon to fly home instead of ride, due to the fact that he was still vomiting and had just healed from that big sore on his shoulder blade. The ride would take nine hours, where the flight would only take two. So Chris and Brandon would fly (I prefer to keep my feet on the ground if I have the option) and Keith and I would drive the van. We would then drive the van to the airport to pick them up the next day.

So we said good-bye to Brandon and Chris, then Keith and I headed out of town to the interstate. Keith was driving and it occurred to me that I hadn't driven since the accident. Three and a half months ago! I told Keith, "Man, I haven't driven in three and a half months, and I've never driven a full size van before. It's going to take some getting used to. I may have to learn how to drive all over again."

With that Keith slowed the van down, pulled over onto the shoulder of the road and said, "You're driving."

"What? No, I didn't say that because I want to drive. You drive!"

"You're driving." Keith is a man of few words.

"No, I'm too scared." I was shaky.

"Then get over here, you're driving."

There was no arguing with Keith. We got out, switched sides and I took a deep breath and pulled out onto the interstate. It was like I was fifteen again, back in Driver's Ed with that white- knuckled grip on the steering wheel. It was nerve-wracking, but I did it. And I'm so thankful that Keith made me. There were going to be a lot of "firsts" that I would have to face over the next couple of months. I needed to be pushed to find courage.

We pulled into our home town, and crossed the 12th Street Bridge. Immediately my eyes went to that embankment, then down to the water. I could almost picture the accident in mind. It made me shudder. The accident happened only about three blocks from home.

As we made the curve towards our driveway, I saw a handicap ramp on the front of our house! Someone had already built it for us and Brandon would be able to get in the house without any trouble. It gave me a chest pain. This was our home now, our life now. We pulled into the driveway and there sat Brandon's truck. I didn't want to be here. I didn't want to remember what our life was, what we had, who we were. Somehow, I wished it could've all been different.

Keith got in his car and headed for home and I went into the house and met the "ghosts," the memories of the past. I walked into the kitchen and heard the conversation that I had with the kids about finding something meaningful or life-changing to do with our summer. I remembered the counter being covered with ingredients and dishes to make Yum Yum bars. It was all clean now. As I walked through the front room towards the hall, I noticed that they had widened the sewing room doorway and hung a wider door too. This would become Brandon's temporary bedroom until the addition was built. It looked so small in comparison to the room he had at rehab. I took my luggage to the bedroom and wished my husband could have been there to hold me. I hurt, all over. I threw myself on the bed and cried. It was total self-pity. "Why me Lord, why Brandon, why us? I don't want this to be my life, our life. Why, why, why?"

And then I heard the front door open, "Hello, is anybody here?" It was Renelle. I jumped up off the bed, wiped my tears and ran to the front room to meet her. Her friends had brought her home to stay. I put my arms around her and didn't ever want to let her go again. It was so good to be reunited once again.

We spent the evening talking about the events of the last week and Renelle told me that our home school group had made plans to greet Brandon at the airport. It sounded like there was going to be quite a crowd there to welcome him home. I was so happy for him. It would be such a warm, welcome surprise for him to see everyone there!

In the morning we headed for the airport. I was still a little nervous driving that big van, especially through the city. I found the handicap parking area, which I had never used before now and parked the van. We went to the gate that Brandon would be arriving at and there were already people there to greet him. It was so nice to see all of our friends again and to see their excitement for Brandon to come home. The local newspaper was even there to do a story about his home coming.

Soon their plane arrived and we all anxiously awaited Brandon's appearance. Since he is in a wheelchair, he had to exit last. So after everyone else was off we waited, and waited, and waited. Finally here they came! Chris was pushing Brandon in his yellow manual chair and Brandon looked so surprised, he looked pale. He didn't look like he felt good at all. His friends were greeting him and they had balloons and gifts and even a basketball that was signed by his teammates. They were all so happy and excited that he was back. But Brandon looked miserable. He wanted to get out of there, get away from everybody and be alone. He wasn't expecting this at all, and he wasn't anywhere near ready to deal with it.

I thanked everyone for their kindness and thoughtfulness and apologized that Brandon had been sick and wasn't feeling good and we needed to get him home. So we headed straight for the van, loaded up and headed for home.

I felt bad that we weren't more joyous and receptive of everyone's good cheer. We just didn't have the strength or the desire to celebrate. We were about to embark on our "new normal" with all the frightening unknowns out there, and we couldn't find it in ourselves to be celebratory. I prayed they would all understand.

A New Normal

CONSTRUCTION was beginning. They tore down our one car garage to make room for a two car garage, tall enough to house our new van with the raised roof. They would be going out from our tiny kitchen with a new family room and a large bedroom. One side of his bedroom would be made into an office, with a desk designed just for Brandon's needs. There would also be a handicap accessible bathroom, complete with a roll-in shower, a sink that he could roll under and most importantly, two heat lamps.

With Brandon's limited sensation, he can only feel heat and cold from the neck up, so if his nose, neck, or his ears are cold, he's cold all over. These heat lamps would make all the difference between an enjoyable shower and a miserable one. I tried to imagine once what it would be like to only feel heat and cold from the neck up, but every time I tried it, I could only feel how cold my toes were. It's hard to disconnect sensation when you have it. We would all have to learn to be sympathetic to his discomfort, because he will sit with a heater blowing full steam ahead most of the winter to try to stay comfortable. All the while the rest of us are burning up.

We lived in a modest ranch style house, with the main living area being in the basement. It had a very small kitchen, with barely enough room for a table and chairs, a small front room (I never could quite figure out what the builder was thinking when he designed it. It's really too small to be any kind of a living room) three bedrooms and a bath room. So all four of us would be spending the majority of our time in this small front room until the addition was done.

Brandon had the smallest of the three bedrooms, because it had the easiest turn to make into the room. It was a very tight fit for his hospital bed and had just enough room to be able to pull his wheelchair up to the side of it. Plus, poor guy, I had just decorated the whole room with sunflowers. I had done a pretty yellow faux finish on the top half of the wall, and dark green faux finish on the bottom half and dividing the two was a beautiful sunflower border. I had made a cute sunflower balloon valance to hang in the window. It was my sewing room. My happy place. Not Brandon's favorite choice of decor. But he put up with it, because he knew it was temporary.

We would spend our days just sitting in that front room, doing school, talking or watching TV. I tried to make sure we got out of the house at least once a day, even if it was just for a half price drink during Happy Hour at our local Sonic. When it was volleyball and basketball season, I coached the volleyball team and assisted with the basketball team and Renelle played, so we would all go to practices and games together. A year later, Brandon would help assist with the boys basketball team. We almost enjoyed it, but it would never be the same. Our love for the game was not as intense as it was before the accident. We loved the kids more than anything and enjoyed coaching and teaching them, and that is what drove us. Brandon only helped one year. He felt as though he couldn't speak loud enough to be heard, and because of his limited air intake he is very soft spoken. It was a nice way to get out of that tiny house and see friends. Just having two rooms accessible to Brandon was hard to get used to after having the run of the huge medical complex at rehab.

Night times took a little more for me to get used to. Again, it was like bringing home my newborn and half-listening all night to hear if it was still breathing. We put in baby monitors so I could hear him if he needed anything. Later, we decided those weren't really necessary, he could yell loud enough if he needed to.

The other really odd thing was every morning, for the longest time, I would wake up like it was in the past, and everything was OK, normal, and it wasn't until I came to full consciousness that it would dawn on me that Brandon was paralyzed. It was like a new reminder each and every morning. I would say to myself, "Oh yeah, Brandon's paralyzed." I was so glad when that finally stopped happening, it was like a new trauma every day.

Since I was now in control of his medical decisions I pulled the new medication, the one I suspected, out of his daily meds. The very first day, Brandon could tell a difference. He didn't vomit. He still had no appetite, but at least he didn't vomit. The next day he felt better yet, and actually ate a little something for lunch. I never put that pill back into his pill box. I threw the awful thing away! Next, I would take him off the second stomach pill. I would ask him if he felt sick, and no, he felt fine. Second one went in the trash. The third one was solely for acid reflux and that one we kept him on a little longer. We monitored his weight, his bowels and how he felt and he was doing so much better. He could actually be up and around and not feel yucky all day. And food was beginning to taste good again! Not too much longer, that third pill was thrown away too. He was down to the absolute essential pills—the one for his nerve pain and one for bladder spasms. It felt so good to get those unneeded chemicals out of his body.

Brandon had a home health aide that would come to the house every morning to do some stretching exercises on Brandon and would get him up and bathed. This was a tremendous help to me. Cindy became part of the family. I could sleep in, and she would come in and take care of Brandon's needs. I still thank the Lord for her to this day. She was so reliable and helpful and genuinely compassionate. She was a God-send to our family. He would have other aides on the weekends and on Cindy's days off, and they were all so helpful and caring. We appreciated every one of them.

One particular day Brandon was feeling especially down. People would often ask if he was depressed. Yes, he was down, but not despondent. Everyone has to deal with some level of depression in their lives and Brandon's had been taken to a whole new level. On this day, he had no desire to get up out of bed. When Cindy was leaving she told me, "He's really depressed this morning and didn't even want me to wash his face. I don't know what you would like me to do."

"Thanks anyway, Cindy. I think I'll just let him stay in bed today."

When she left, I went into Brandon's room and he had the sheet pulled up over his head. (This is his normal way of sleeping. It keeps his nose warm). I pulled the sheet back, his eyes were closed, but I could see a tear in the very corner.

"Are you sick?" I asked.

He shook his head.

"Are you just having a bad day?"

He nodded his head.

I pulled open the blinds and let the sunshine in.

"Would you keep those closed, please?" He requested.

I closed them. I could tell this was going to be a despondent day. I went over to the side of the bed and pulled his sheet back again. I had tears, but I would not let them fall.

"You know what, son? If anybody in this world deserves a day to feel sorry for himself, it's you! I'm going let you stay in this bed, with the blinds and the door closed, all day if you want. You deserve it." It was taking all I had within me not to break down.

"But tomorrow, we're going to open the blinds, you're going to get out of that bed, get dressed and we are going to go on." I gave him a big hug and a kiss on his forehead.

"I know this is not easy, but we can do this. It will get better, it has to. We have to believe that it will. But today, just sleep, and cry if you want to. You need to! I will keep the door closed and not bother you, but if you call me, I'll be right here. I love you, son."

I kissed him again, we both had tears and I left the room, closing the door behind me. Then I let the tears flow freely. I asked the Lord to comfort him, to put His arms around him and give him peace. I asked Him to encourage his heart in some way and give him a desire to live, to go on, and to make a life for himself. But my heart was breaking once again for my son.

It wasn't until late in the day that Brandon hollered my name. He needed his next dose of pills. He looked better, but still wanted to stay in bed. And he did, all day. We talked about all that he'd lost, that would never be regained, and let ourselves be sad about it. But tomorrow was going to be a new day. We would have to make an extra special effort to find things to be thankful for.

The construction crew was busy working to get the addition done by Thanksgiving. How appropriate! We'd have so much to give thanks for! The builder was asking me what kind of flooring I wanted, what kind of trim, what color of paint? So many decisions, yet I had no desire whatsoever to make them. I just told him to make the addition look like it belongs on the rest of the house and I'd be fine with that. He made wonderful choices. Brandon had a HUGE picture window in his bedroom, so even if he was indoors, it felt like he was outdoors. They built him an armoire that had pop open doors so it was easily accessible. They put two big windows in the family room and had neutral paint colors on the walls. It was perfect. It had a deck out the back door, which became Brandon's favorite spot for sun-bathing. We moved right in as soon as it was done and our home now felt ten times bigger.

Renelle asked Brandon is she could move into his old room in the basement, king size waterbed and all. Of course, he said yes. We turned Renelle's old bedroom into a guest room and my old sewing room became Chris' office. I had no desire anymore to sew. The kitchen felt so much bigger since that is where the addition was put on. We were so grateful. I always felt like it was God's house, He gave it to us. One time someone said how lucky we were to have an addition put on, for free! I gently reminded that person that Brandon paid a very dear price for that addition. It definitely wasn't free, just because insurance paid for it.

One morning I turned on the morning news to hear a report about this drug that the FDA had pulled from the

The deck was built off of this back door.

market and was banned. Several people had died from it and several were critically ill. I turned the TV up. They went on to name that drug and it was the one that Brandon had been taking that I threw away! The one that had made him so sick! I knew it! I asked Brandon, "Did you hear that?" I had to stop and thank God that He protected Brandon from death or permanent harm from that drug. He could've died! I thought, should I call his doctor and tell him? No, he would surely know. I would wait for him to call me, after all he didn't know for sure I had taken Brandon off of that pill. I waited. It never happened. He never called to tell me to throw that bottle of pills away. But when we went back to the rehab hospital for Brandon's one year re-evaluation, I made sure to mention it to his doctor and all he said was, "Yeah, sorry about that." That's why I dislike pharmaceuticals. Easy to give, easy to walk away from the responsibility of. All those endless days of puking because of some raunchy medication that our pharmaceutical companies could profit off of at his expense. Maddening.

Life was moving on. We decided it would be best for Brandon to go to the local learning center and take whatever classes were necessary for him to get his GED, instead of trying to home school. He finished well and his instructor asked him to be the speaker at his graduation. I was so proud of him! He gave a speech about being transformed. About how a caterpillar builds a cocoon and then it has to struggle to break free from that cocoon. And if anyone helped it break free from that tough chrysalis, its wings would be too weak to fly and it would die. It needed the struggle to strengthen its wing, so it could fly away a beautiful butterfly. All I could think about was Brandon and his

Brandon speaking at his graduation.

struggles and how he was emerging as a beautiful butterfly. I was so proud of him.

Chris is an engineer, so he brought some software home and taught Brandon how to do drafting and engineering work on his computer, using his track ball mouse. He was a natural. He caught on so easily and was so proficient at it, that it wasn't long and he got a job working with Chris. They would both get up in the morning and go to work together. Chris would be there to help him out with whatever need arose and Brandon could get out in the real world and be productive. It was a wonderful thing.

Renelle and I accelerated her school work and she would actually graduate from high school a year early. She continued to play ball and I continued to coach volleyball and Chris and I coached girls basketball. And once Renelle graduated she would be my assistant volleyball coach. We were adjusting to our new normal very well.

The two year window came and went and Brandon never did regain any movement or sensation below his level of injury. We often wondered if the Sygen came too late, or if he actually had the placebo. It seemed like a very missed opportunity, but we still had to believe that God is the one who is ultimately in control. If He wanted to heal him, He would. We just needed to keep and practice the faith. Some would say that our faith wasn't strong enough, some would say God was punishing us for some reason. I remember being asked if Brandon was being punished for his sin, and I said, "Why isn't your son in a wheelchair? Has your son never sinned? Why am I not in a wheelchair? I am one of the biggest sinners there is! I should be dead! God should've killed me for all of my willful disobedience! Why are any of us up walking around at all?" I was beginning to identify Job's friends. We all have them, and we have to love them anyway.

Our new normal was really becoming quite OK. We found joy in the simplest things. Our priority list from the past was completely obliterated and laughable. Why did we make the things that were *so important*, important in the first place? We were once again enjoying life and finding laughter and peace in our home. Brandon's health had improved greatly! He had gained weight, strength and confidence in his new body.

He began to get bored with his plain powerchair and decided it needed some soupin' up. So he designed a new knob out of stainless steel that was far better than the plastic one that came with the chair. He actually had several of these manufactured and a company in the next big city sold several to their clients who were also powerchair owners. It was always so fun to see someone riding in their chair and recognize the knob as Brandon's design. But the knob wasn't enough; he put blue lights under his chair, and even designed spinners, made from polished aluminum for the wheels. I have to admit, it looked much cooler when he was done. I tried to encourage him to market those too, but they would be too expensive for most of the people riding in chairs, since the majority live on very fixed incomes.

Brandon was ready for a new adventure. It had been five years since his accident and he was ready to try college. He found a community college about an hour away that offered the engineering courses that he was interested in. After much investigation, he decided to give it a try.

College Days

NOW PREPARING for college was a lot of work. Brandon did all of his own research and preparations to make it happen. He had to make sure his dorm room was handicap accessible, he had to find a roommate that could help him with some of his needs, and he had to find a home health agency that would come to the school morning and evening to get him up and ready for class and be able to put him to bed at night. And he needed help in the classroom to get the work done. That's a much different "to do" list in comparison to most college students.

For me, I was excited for him, that he was willing to take this huge step in independence, but on the other hand I was scared of the unknowns. I was once again in control of his environment, how clean his living quarters were, how healthy his meals were, how well groomed he was, how clean his clothes were, his bowel program was closely monitored, his skin was closely watched for sores, and I knew when he was struggling and helped to find solutions. Now that is *a lot* of control! I was going to have to give all of that up! And that wasn't easy!

We got through the enrollment and toured part of the school. Some of his classes were on the second floor and the only access points were these outside elevators. I use that term loosely, because they were more like lifts. They were completely out in the open on the outside of the building and someone would have to come and open the door for him to let him in or out of the building. I was ready to nix the whole plan when I saw these. They looked old and rusty and totally unreliable. I just didn't like them. But, I had to give up control and let Brandon run his own life and this was the school that offered the classes that he wanted. So there was no other option.

Next, we went to the home health agency in this particular town. Now, I don't mean any disrespect whatsoever to people who are home health aides. There are many wonderful, thorough and caring aides out there working in this field. And we were blessed to know a few. But we were about to find out that there are many who are lazy, unreliable and only do this job because they aren't fit to do anything else. Those of you who have had to use home health aides will know what I mean. We hired the agency, gave them Brandon's schedule, along with a list of needs that he had, and they agreed to take him on. This was the hardest area for me to yield control in, because it was detrimental to Brandon's well-being.

The dorm room that he had was roomy enough, just concrete block walls, a window and two beds. A young man from our home school group, that played basketball with Brandon, agreed to be his roommate. That gave me some peace of mind. Just knowing he would have a friend with him, to look out for him. It also had a small bathroom with a toilet, a sink, and a shower, that they would share with the boys next door. I wondered how sanitary it would be.

We headed for home, double checking our list to make sure that we had thought of everything Brandon would need before the big move. I wanted him to come home on the weekends since it was only an hour away. That way I could do his laundry and make sure he was at least getting healthy meals two days a week. I would pick him up on Fridays after class and bring him back on Sunday nights.

A friend of Brandon's roommate offered to help with the move. So we loaded his van and our van and made our way to college. I had butterflies in my stomach because I was nervous for Brandon. We got him all unpacked and moved in. I made his bed, put away his clothes and medical supplies, and then Brandon told me, "Don't worry about the rest. I'll take care of it." Not what I wanted to hear. I wanted to hear, "Don't go, I can't do this without you. Please stay and help me." But, I had to let go. I had to realize that my son was ready to be independent, that he didn't want to have to rely on his parents anymore and that he was a man and he could take care of himself. Such a mixture of emotions, bursting with pride at his maturity, yet crushed that I wasn't needed.

Of course I couldn't hold him and cry my eyes out in front of his friends—that would be humiliating—so I gave him a hug, a slight peck on the forehead and told him to work hard and learn a lot. I stayed positive and kept a smile on my face. I hugged his roommate and thanked him for being there for Brandon, and we left.

We weren't even in the van yet and I couldn't hold back the flood. I boo-hooed all the way home. Poor Chris just kept giving me the sympathetic eye, and reminding me that everything was going to be fine and that we should be happy that Brandon had made this huge step. I was happy. Some of the tears were happy tears. Most of them were proud tears, proud of all that he had made it through and never gave up. I never doubted for one minute that he wouldn't make it. He is very strong-willed when he makes his mind up. I just didn't want anything to be a barrier to his success and happiness.

After the excitement of the first two weeks the difficult reality began to set in. His roommate would have a much different schedule than Brandon, so they wouldn't see each other much. Brandon still had difficulty asking strangers for help, so meal time was very scarce and it had to be something he could eat without assistance. Nothing that needed to be cut up into smaller pieces or peeled or mashed. The outdoor elevators would quit when Brandon was only half-way up to the second level and his teachers would notice that he wasn't in class and they would go looking for him and find him stranded on the elevators. And the home health aides were unreliable. It was proving to be quite a challenge.

One night at 4:00 a.m. our phone rang.

"Mom, I think my catheter is blocked," Brandon said.

I was still trying to get my senses together from a dead sleep.

"Are you hyper-reflexing?" I ask. (That's when blood pressure sky rockets due to a full bladder.)

"I think so. Plus, I can hear urine pouring into a puddle in my bed."

I quietly listened, and I could hear it too, over the phone.

"Did you call the home health agency?"

"Yeah, they can't get anyone here until 8:00 a.m."

"What? Don't they have an emergency number?"

"That is the emergency number. Do you think you or dad could come and change my tube?"

I calculate in my head: If I leave now I could be there around 5:00 a.m.—that's still three hours sooner than an aide.

"Of course! I'll get there as soon as I can."

When I walked in, poor Brandon was lying in a pool of urine. I didn't know what to do first. I wanted to rescue him from the cesspool, but it wouldn't help until his catheter was changed. So he laid in his own urine while I changed out his tube. Then I began the challenge of sopping up the pool with towels and dirty laundry, anything I could find, so that I could take the sheets off, out from under him, get him on a dry surface, clean him up and dress him, and then clean up his bed. Thankfully his mattress had a water proof covering, so it wasn't sopped. It made me so angry that he had to endure this! What good is a home health agency if you can't rely on them to help you in a time of trouble?

Brandon kept telling me to calm down. It's not that big of deal. He lived through it. But my thought was: What if it had been something more serious? I wanted to wait until 8:00 a.m., so I could give the aide a piece of my mind, but Brandon wouldn't let me. He told me that he would take care of it and to quit worrying about it. He thanked me for coming and said I could leave. It wasn't easy, but I did. I gathered up all the soaking wet laundry, put it in a garbage bag and headed for home.

There would be several aides during his year at college. It was the most challenging part of his whole college experience. Maybe if he were in a bigger town with more population he could've found a more reliable service.

During the semester break, Brandon came home for those two weeks. I could tell by the way his clothes were fitting that he'd lost weight. I also discovered a sore that was starting on his bottom. He was somewhat discouraged with all the challenges and, with winter, being stuck outside on the elevators was a dangerous problem. He was considering quitting.

We all discussed it, tried to find solutions and encouraged Brandon to stick it out and finish the first year at least. He wasn't too excited about it, but he agreed. If he didn't finish now, he might never finish.

He went back to school and pushed through the winter. On really cold and snowy days, he would skip the classes that he had to use the elevator and make up for it later. The ladies that worked in the cafeteria took it upon themselves to see to it that Brandon started eating better. And eventually, after firing several, he found a semi-reliable aide. So he was finding his own way through the struggles.

When spring arrived it was so much better. However the sore on his bottom was looking a whole lot worse. When he was at home, with his excellent aide, she discovered that it was much deeper than it appeared and recommended that we have the nurse come and look at it. After the nurse's inspection, she found out that it was actually tunneling. That means the hole was worming its way down to the bone. She recommended making an appointment with the surgeon.

The surgeon did a thorough exam, and it was a lot worse than how it looked. To look at it, it looked no bigger than a pencil eraser. It was really red all the way around the hole, but it didn't look terrible. He said the flesh was almost completely detached from his butt bone and told us it might require a skin flap surgery. The surgeon was not real positive about the surgery because it can actually cause other issues for his skin. He recommended that Brandon stay in bed until it healed. However long it took.

As soon as school was out, Brandon went to bed. The home health nurse would come out every day to change the packing and the dressing. It was so deep she could stuff a four foot strip of narrow gauze into that little hole. We got to see firsthand the danger that was always preached to us at the rehab hospital. Sores can happen so quickly and be so bad before you are even aware of them.

He would end up spending seven months in that bed. We figured out a way for him to be able to get on a laptop while he was in bed, and of course he had the TV, but seven months is a long time. The strips of gauze the nurse was stuffing in the sore were getting shorter, that was a good sign. We were filling his meals with lots of protein and calories to accelerate healing. Insurance even provided an air bed, where he had no pressure points anywhere on his body while he was lying in it. Friends would come to see him and watch TV with him, which was so nice and helped to pass the time in a more fun way. Eventually we would let him get out of bed for a few hours a day just so he wouldn't lose all his strength and mobility, and then gradually increased it when the sore was almost healed. If the gauze strips looked bloody or got longer, back in bed he'd have to stay. It was a long seven months, but it healed up just fine and it didn't require surgery. I'm so thankful he had a wise surgeon to make this decision.

So after much debate and discussion he decided that one year of college was all his health could afford. While all the other kids worry about what party to attend or whether or not they would make the team or which club should they join, Brandon had much different choices to consider.

People used to always say, "He's going to go to college isn't he?" If they only knew.

Moving Out

BRANDON WAS hired by a company to do some work from home drawing electrical schematics. He does this on the computer using his track ball mouse. This job was such a blessing. I was so grateful when a job opportunity presented itself to Brandon and the person doing the interview saw the "ability" in Brandon, rather than the "disability." Even now that he's in a wheelchair, he still has a tremendous work ethic and he doesn't put off work until the last minute. If a project needed done in a timely manner, Brandon would have it done before the deadline.

It was a small income, but a steady income, and with the help he got from Social Security, he figured he could afford to live on his own. I had such mixed emotions about this. I knew it had to happen sooner or later and I knew that Brandon was ready. However, I had been his main caregiver for the past seven years and not having that responsibility left me feeling very empty. I had my kids with me twenty four hours a day seven days a week my entire marriage—with homeschooling and care giving my only passions. The empty nest looked very dark and dismal.

He was busy doing research to find a place that suited his needs. When he found one, it was thirty minutes away. "That's too far!" I thought to myself. I wanted him to stay in the same town as us. Brandon was excited to check it all out. I wasn't excited, but I knew I better get that way.

The apartment was located in a handicap-accessible housing development. It was gated with security guards and all the apartments were built with handicap accessibility in every way. In the main building they had rooms for those with more severe disabilities—residents who required more nursing care. It was a lot more cheery than a nursing home, but still not what I had envisioned for my son. I never wanted to see him have to settle for nursing home care.

The area of town was not too far from shopping, dining and doctors offices. But the traffic was a lot heavier than what we were used to. They had several crosswalks and all sidewalks had curb cutouts. There were definitely a lot more opportunities for Brandon to get out and about and enjoy his independence.

Having the college experience really prepared him for the obstacles he might have to face in being totally independent. He would again have to find reliable home health care. Since this was a totally handicap housing area, it proved to be much easier to find. Jackie, his home health aide, has always been a phone call away no matter what time of day it is. She has been such a great peace-giver to me. And Brandon can call on her for anything and she is there. She is wonderful!

His apartment was a small one bedroom with a bathroom and a roll-in shower, a small family room and a kitchenette. We built him a desk by copying the desk the builders designed for his addition and put it in his family room. It was small, but it was cozy. He had everything he needed right at his reach. I wrote a message on his memo board, "Call your mom!" I didn't want him to completely forget about me. I knew I was going to miss him terribly. I reminded him that we were only thirty minutes away if he ever needed anything at all, call.

Moving him this time was a lot different than moving him to college. This was permanent. Again, my emotions were mixed. Renelle had already moved out and was making a life for herself and now the nest was going to be totally empty. I knew that Brandon had learned and matured so much from all of life's experiences that he was definitely ready and able to do this. I was not as worried about his environment this time since it was all designed for people with disabilities, so all the way around it was easier to let him go. However, mothers never quit worrying about their kids.

One day I was in his city to do some shopping and I was sitting at a stop light where the intersection is one of the busiest in this city. All of a sudden I saw a wheelchair speeding through the huge intersection to beat the red light, and it's my son! Power wheelchairs can go about 7.5 mph. I closed my eyes and prayed that he would always be safe riding around in that big city. He didn't see me, but seeing him reminded me that I was not in control. I knew that there would be many dangers and temptations, but I had to trust that Brandon knew the right decisions to make.

Since he lives in this big city he is able to ride his chair to most of his doctor's appointments. One day as he was entering a doctor's office his size 14 shoe got hung up on the door frame. Brandon cannot see his feet because he cannot lean forward so he was unaware that his foot was stuck. He proceeded to make the turn and enter the office and his leg twisted and broke free of the door frame and his leg was dangling off the foot rest. He couldn't feel anything so he just had someone lift his foot and put it back on its foot rest.

Later that night when Jackie was putting him to bed she noticed that his leg was all red and swollen. She asked him what happened and he didn't know for sure. All he could think of was the incident at the doctor's office and that he had heard a "pop."

The next day they went to the emergency room, got an x-ray, and sure enough he had broken his leg. His tibia had a clean crack all the way through. When I think about the pain that he would have felt, I was grateful that he didn't feel a thing. They put him in a cast and we prayed that it would heal without needing any kind of a surgery. The doctor reminded us that since it will never be weight bearing, it didn't need to be pinned or anything. That was good to know, that surgery wasn't necessary, but another painful reminder that Brandon would never walk again. In some way, I almost wished that Brandon would've felt pain. It would've been a sign for hope.

Life at home was quiet. Too quiet! His side of the house was empty, lonely. I moved my dining room table and chairs into his family room, which freed up my kitchen. Then I moved the family room furniture into his bedroom. His bathroom became my bathroom and Chris had the other one all to himself. It didn't look empty anymore, but it still felt empty.

For a couple of weeks, after he moved out, I would be in bed asleep and I would wake up to hear him calling me from his room. He would call out in the middle of the night sometimes if his catheter was blocked or if he needed something. I would have to remind myself that he was gone.

Still other times I would get up and realize that I was only dreaming. It took some time for it to all settle in my mind that he was gone.

I would, at least once a week, take my lunch break with him. I had to check in and make sure that he was doing well. Just talking on the phone or instant messaging wasn't good enough. I had to see him with my own two eyes to be sure that everything was all right. And it was, very good.

He was living life to the fullest that he could live it. He went parasailing once on Table Rock Lake with his sister and some friends. He overcame his fear of water. Later, Chris and I took him on a trip to South Carolina. There he got to parasail in Charleston Bay. He even made the evening news in Charleston that night, "Paralyzed Man Parasails in Charleston Bay." We made it back to the hotel just in time to see him on the news. I hoped and prayed that the news story inspired some other paralyzed person to be courageous enough to give it a try.

Brandon began doing some research to find a canine companion. At the start of his search he thought it would be really cool to get a monkey. And what a chick magnet it would be! But upon further research he realized that it would be a lot of work for his aide to do, and he didn't want to do that to her. So he decided that a dog would be much easier to care for. It would be very helpful for him to have a companion that could pick up his phone if he dropped it on the floor, or anything for that matter that landed on the floor, his remote, his wallet, CDs, even paper. He signed up to be considered for a dog and was accepted. Now for training.

The agency and the training were about three hours away, so he would have to go out of town to attend the classes the first week and spend the second week in class with the dog, getting to know each other and learning how to give all of the commands to get the dog to respond. Then the last night of training the dog would go home with him and spend the night before they went home together.

His first dog was Trey. He was a Doberman, and a very big boy. He never really got accustomed to Brandon's little apartment and he liked to run. One night he escaped out the door and Brandon's aide looked for him until 2:00 a.m. That dog ran for hours! He ended up having to give Trey back, and let him go to a different job. He just wasn't a good fit.

Next there was Alex. Alex was a beautiful long haired, blonde golden retriever. She was the sweetest dog and very good at picking up anything that Brandon dropped. She could even pick up small pieces of paper! I have to admit that I somewhat spoiled her, she wanted lovin' and I gave it to her. That's a no-no with a working dog. Brandon would scold me and tell me that I was ruining her. I couldn't help it. It was a very good thing that I didn't see her often.

One of the negatives about a long, blonde golden retriever is the hair. It would become the responsibility of the aide to brush her. And Alex left her hair all over the apartment. The floor was covered, the couch was covered and the air was always afloat with her golden fluff. That was something that we didn't really consider before hiring her. It became too much to deal with. and he eventually had to return her also. She now resides in Lima, Peru with another family. She was a great dog.

I was so proud of Brandon. He had overcome so many obstacles and was really adjusting very well to being independent. I am also very proud to say that he never had to ask us for financial assistance. That is very commendable for a young handicapped man to handle his finances so well that he was always able to pay his own bills! And, he could even afford to take care of some of his wants and even help others financially! How someone on a fixed budget is able to do this is extraordinary!

He amazes me all the time with his level of confidence, maturity, responsibility and contentment. If I was in his chair, I don't think I'd be half the person he is. I know the Lord saved his life for a reason. He's such an inspiration to me. If he can get out of bed every day, pay his bills, help someone in need and be content, then I have nothing to complain about or have an excuse to give.

Brandon made many new friends living in the city—many of them were his own neighbors. He helped them whenever he could, however he could. He also made friends with many of the employees of the housing area and managers too. One day we called him to see if he could go out to dinner with us. "Yeah, sure! Do you mind if I bring a friend? I have someone I'd like you to meet."

A Wedding

ON THE WAY to Brandon's apartment, I'm asking Chris, "Who do you suppose Brandon is bringing to dinner?" I am the kind of person that will try to solve a mystery instead of waiting to find out when I get there. "Let's see, we've met his best friend Ben, and he's joined us several times for dinner or a movie, so it can't be him." I'm running through my mind trying to think of people that he's mentioned on the phone or just in passing. The curiosity is about to eat me alive! Chris just says, "You'll find out when we get there." What a fuddy duddy. There's no fun in waiting!

We pull up to his apartment and his door opens and out he rolls with a lady walking behind him. I didn't recognize her, it wasn't his aide.

"Mom, Dad, this is Tammy." Brandon says.

"Hello, nice to meet you!" We shake her hand.

We load up in Brandon's van and head off to the restaurant. I'm thinking: Is she a friend? Or is she a "Friend"? You know, a girlfriend! My heart skipped a beat at the thought of him having a girlfriend.

So all evening I'm doing my best not to read anything into this relationship, not to jump to conclusions, and to remain as neutral as possible. This is *not* easy for me to do. She told us that she drove the buses at the housing complex. She took the residents to appointments, to work and to shopping centers or to any place else they needed transportation, and had been doing this for several years. So she'd known Brandon for a long time. I was finding myself liking her. She seemed very thoughtful and considerate. But I was still scolding myself saying, "She's just a friend of Brandon's—that is all. Don't read anything into this."

We had a very enjoyable dinner together and we drove back to Brandon's apartment. We said our good-byes, nice to meet yous and headed for home. I started in with questioning Chris, "*So*, what do you think?"

"What do I think of what?"

"What do you think of Tammy?"

"She's nice!"

"Do you think there is more than just friendship there?"

"Honey, you're always reading more into things than what is there."

"Well, it has to mean something that he wanted us to meet her, don't you think?"

"Not necessarily."

"Brandon treated her like more than just a friend, I thought."

"You would think that."

"So you think it was just wishful thinking on my part?"

"I don't know. I know that you think too much."

He's no fun. He can never read between the lines or figure things out before they happen. He's way too practical. He keeps me balanced, I guess. I was going to go ahead and think that she was more than just a friend because I had that Mother's Knot. My gut was telling me so. I could see it in Brandon's face.

Now, to make a long and private story short, I was right! They were more than just friends! Tammy told me one day that when she looks at Brandon she doesn't even see his chair. That is exactly what I had been praying for! Someone who would love Brandon just the way he is. Tammy never knew Brandon any other way. She's never seen him walk or run. She's never felt him squeeze her hand. She's never seen how tall he stands or seen him use his hands. She loves him just like he is. As his mom, I couldn't ask for anything more. She's perfect for my son and I love her for loving him.

It wasn't long after that, Brandon proposed. She accepted and wedding plans were in the making. Their wedding was absolutely beautiful! Everything about it was perfect. They chose a botanical garden for the site. Chris officiated the service, his voice only cracking once. Brandon's two best friends were his groomsmen, and Tammy's two daughters were her bridesmaids. Tammy's son-in-law walked her down the aisle, her granddaughter was the flower girl, and her grandson was the ring bearer. The union of two families and the union of a sweet couple. It was a day that I always hoped and prayed that we would see.

For their first anniversary, Tammy set up a surprise flight for Brandon. Tammy's son-in-law, John, is in the Air Force and has a friend who is a pilot at a base in the city where they live. They worked out a surprise plan for Brandon to be able to fly in the co-pilot's seat. It was a dream come true for Brandon. And for us, as his parents, to see him so happy, was such a blessing. We love the fact that Tammy is so thoughtful and considerate of Brandon. And Brandon is equally thoughtful and considerate of Tammy.

Knowing that they have each other, through thick and thin, is such a wonderful thing to watch. I pray always that their lives will be blessed and they will have many happy years together.

Presenting Mr. & Mrs. Brandon and Tammy Coleman

Tammy being walked down the aisle by her son-in-law, John.

Tammy and her beautiful bridesmaid daughters, Kristy on the left and Anna on the right.

Chris presided over the wedding vows.

The wonderful grandkids! Kaitlyn was
the flower girl, and Jonathan was the
ring bearer.

The wedding party. Brandon's best friend Jed, standing to the right of the flower girl, and Ben sitting behind him, were the groomsmen.

Brandon with his two grandmas. Ruth on the left and Fanny on the right.

Brandon and Renelle

Double Knot

I DID A LITTLE bit of research on knots. I was surprised to find that there are hundreds of them. Most of them are used in mountain climbing and marine life. A knot is a method in fastening or securing linear material, such as rope, by tying or interweaving it to itself or some other object. A Mother's Knot is a *knowing*—an intuition used in securing a child or anyone with whom you have a relationship.

Some would call it a mother's intuition. Others would say, "I have eyes in the back of my head!" It's that gut feeling that something is amiss. I remember countless times as a child tip toeing to the kitchen and ever so silently opening the cookie jar. With a cookie in one hand, I would very gently lower the lid back on the cookie jar with the other hand, only to hear my mom say, "You're going to ruin your supper! Put that back!" How did she know? She wasn't anywhere to be seen! She couldn't have heard anything, I was completely silent! She would always say, "I have eyes in the back of my head." I never could see them, but I knew they were there because she caught me numerous times.

It's a gift that God gives to mothers to help them protect their children from hurt, harm or danger. Many times when Brandon and Renelle were little, it would be very quiet in the house and immediately I would get this little knot in my gut that something needed my immediate attention. I would go to their room to find them coloring on the walls with their new crayons, or tearing pages from their story books, or dumping lotion out on the floor. Nothing terrible, yet something destructive none the less.

I was always very sensitive to that *knowing*. As the kids got older and I wasn't always in the next room to run and check on them, I would pray for them. Whenever that knot appeared and I had no idea why, I would use it as a signal to pray—either for their safety or for wisdom for them to make a wise decision. It became a knot that fastened me to our heavenly Father. I would run to Him and say, "Check on the kids, something's wrong!" Of course, He always knew right where they were and exactly what they were doing. It was more of a reminder for me that God is in control. He sees and knows everything all the time.

I used to question why God gave me that Mother's Knot that fateful morning. For years I felt that God didn't hear me or answer my prayers because Brandon wasn't protected from harm. I was angry at God. I remember when I was a child letting my best friend play with my favorite toy, trusting her to return it in one piece. And when she returned it, it was broken and had pieces missing! I never trusted her again with my stuff. That was how I felt toward God. I had entrusted Him with my precious child, and He returned him to me broken.

But looking back on everything that happened, I know God was there. Someone once said, "Just imagine what could've happened if you didn't pray." And then I would feel this awesome load of responsibility that I could not bear to carry. How could God trust *me* to pray when prayer was needed? What if I ignored his promptings? I am nothing, nobody. I possess no special power or special gifts. It all hinged on *my* obedience to pray? That thought is still overwhelming to me today. I cannot and will not believe that the responsibility was on my shoulders and that it was my prayers that saved his life. That is too much responsibility to put on any imperfect human being.

Deuteronomy 32:39 says, "See now that I (God) even I, am He, and there is no god with me: **I kill, I make alive; I wound, and I heal;** neither is there any that can deliver out of my hand." It is God's responsibility, He takes it fully. If it was my prayer that saved Brandon, I could take the credit. I could say, "It was all me, I did this." God would not get the glory, I would.

I believe my burden that day to pray was God preparing me, to help me deal with this tragedy. I believe He had all those people in all the right places way ahead of time. He was trying to prepare me for what was going to happen. He knows my every weakness and fear, and He loves me and knows my need. He is my Father.

To go back and recount all that the Lord did on that day and the days following is both miraculous and humbling. First of all, what if that lady had not been sitting in the drive thru at McDonalds to witness it all? It could have been a very slow time for McDonalds and the drive thru could've been empty. No witness would've meant no 911 call. But she was there, right where Brandon needed her to be.

What if Vern had not been in there drinking coffee with his buddies? What if he had to work through his afternoon break? And what if he had just stood and watched, as the other people did, instead of jumping in the water to save Brandon? But he was there, and he listened to his gut and went into the creek to save Brandon.

What if Brandon hadn't been able to hold his breath for four minutes or more? Brandon told me that night he got off the ventilator, "I believe the Lord held my breath."

The EMS team members that were there that day were recognized as the fastest responders in the state that year. Their expertise was outstanding. They were right there to care for Brandon in those early minutes.

Remember the lady who covered her name tag to tell us not to leave Brandon alone in his room that second night? We found out later that she was actually the daughter-in-law of a very sweet Christian couple who went to church with Chris's mom some years ago! Coincidence? We didn't know her at all, and she didn't know us. It was later that we made that connection. What if she hadn't been on duty that day? What if she would've ignored her gut feeling? She was right where Brandon needed her to be on that particular night.

I know that I should never ignore my gut. That Mother's Knot keeps me tied to my Heavenly Father who sees and knows all things and who loves and cares for us more than we can ever imagine in our human minds. I now try to keep it a double knot, because I need Him more everyday! I never prayed for any of those people to be where they were, I just prayed for Brandon's protection. God took care of everything that fateful day.

Another tremendous blessing and answer to prayer was Brandon's work comp insurance. He clocked in at 1:00 pm and his accident happened at approximately 3:15 pm. He had only been working for this company for two hours and fifteen minutes! What if this accident had happened while he was mowing for a neighbor or a friend? He wouldn't have had the wonderful insurance coverage that he had for his injury! And Pat, his insurance rep, took such good care of all of us, knowing way ahead of us what our needs would be, and she took care of them all so quickly and thoroughly! She definitely was given to us by God.

In mysterious ways God was preparing me for this. I had been discussing with the kids a meaningful way to spend our summer. Something lasting. We needed to find something life changing or inspirational to do. Well, Brandon's accident was definitely life changing, and a huge learning experience. We spent our summer learning about SCI and TBI and meeting people who were facing the same life-changing tragedies in their lives. Not exactly what I had in mind, but it was certainly life changing!

And in my prayer over my ironing board about letting Brandon get a "crotch rocket" and could I live with it if he was permanently injured? God was definitely preparing my heart for this tragedy! I even told the Lord in that prayer that I would care for Brandon for the rest of his life no matter what condition he was in! When I think of the time of day that it was, it was about the exact time of his accident. That still gives me chills. Just to think I was saying those very words when he hit the bottom of that creek!

The devotionals that we read the morning after the accident were both so amazing and appropriate for the trial we were facing. Coincidence? No, I say they were from God. He must have prompted Debbie to grab my Bible and devotionals knowing that I would pick them up and read them that next morning. I'm so thankful she obeyed the prompting!

The eighth grade graduation financial gifts and the bank fund that people gave were also a God-given provision to us. It paid for every plane ticket for Chris and Renelle to come out to the rehab hospital. The Lord knew we were going to have a great need, and He provided before we even asked!

Reflecting back on all of these circumstances, I see God's hand in it all. But why did God let it happen? I believe that God is in control of all things. That He sees and knows everything that is going to happen. But, I do *not* believe that He *makes* them happen. He just *knows*. How can that be? How can He know, but not do anything about it? That is the question. I'm not even going to try to figure out why God does what He does. He is God, and I am not. But I *do* know that he gives even more grace in a tragic situation. It's just up to us to accept that grace and keep our faith and our focus on Him.

I've come to understand that Mother's Knot as the prompting of the Holy Spirit. He's the one who is our mediator between us and God. We are all born with a *knowing* that God is real and that He's out there somewhere. It's up to us to listen to that *gut feeling* or that *prompting* that God gives us. Or we can ignore it, push it away. God gives us the freedom to choose.

Now, I don't want to lead any of you to think that I am in any way perfect. Lord knows I have ignored Him more times than I can remember. I am ashamed at the countless times I have disobeyed that *still small voice* and it amazes me that God would want to communicate with me at all! How many times have I given up on talking to someone who doesn't want to have anything to do with me? Yet the Lord is patient, and kind and He knows that we're made of nothing but dirt, and to dirt we will return. Yet, He desires to speak to us and to reveal Himself to us, if we want to. He doesn't force Himself on us. He leaves it up to us. Isn't that amazing?

I know on May 18, 1999 that God put all the right people in all the right places to work a miracle for His honor and glory, but why He chose us, I still don't understand. So many times I have felt that we have been very poor examples of His grace and his mercy, yet He still continues to provide and to answer our prayers.

I know that one day Brandon will be whole again, and that he will be walking in his new glorified body, when we all get to heaven. I just wish we could have seen it while we are still on this earth. But God has a plan, and He is the one that is in control. I trust Him to know what is best.

I know that the accident totally changed me. All my priorities were completely rearranged and some completely thrown away. I came to understand the truly important things in life and many of the top priorities I had became ridiculousness.

I know it has drawn me closer to the Lord in my personal life. I threw away all religion (that list of dos and don'ts) and ritualistic ideals and clung to Him only. Man's ideas and opinions are just that, man's. They can be so distracting and misleading that it grieves the Holy Spirit. This also causes doubt and robs you of your faith. I am so thankful for all the Lord has done for us throughout this whole life-changing event. I know that He loves us and that He'll never leave us nor forsake us. He has a purpose way beyond what we can comprehend. My faith is in Him alone.

My whole purpose in writing this book was to make known God's work in our lives to all people. I pray that it does.

I will praise thee, O Lord, with my whole heart; I will shew forth all thy marvelous works. Psalm 9:1

An Important Decision

I WOULD like to take a moment and share a very important message with you. Our time on earth is so very short, it is expedient that you make a decision concerning your eternity. The Holy Bible clearly teaches that you have a choice to make, accept Jesus Christ as your Savior and live eternally in heaven with Him, or deny Him and live eternally separated from Him in a literal place called hell. It is my heart's cry that you will choose Jesus.

The Bible says, "These things have I written unto you that believe on the name of the Son of God; that ye may know that ye have eternal life." (I John 5:13) God wants you to know!

"For God so loved the world that He gave His only begotten son that whosoever believeth in Him should not perish but have ever lasting life." (John 3:16)

God's purpose is that we have eternal life!

"The gift of God is eternal life through Jesus Christ the Lord." (Romans 6:23)

Jesus said, "If I go and prepare a place for you, I will

come again, and receive you unto myself, that where I am, there ye may be also." (John 14:3)

The problem that is we are sinners, and sin keeps us from fulfilling God's purpose. "For all have sinned and come short of the glory of God." (Romans 3:23) Do you believe that?

We cannot save ourselves, "Not of works lest any man should boast." (Ephesians 2:9)

And sin has a price that we cannot pay, "For the wages of sin is death." (Romans 6:23)

The good news is that God has provided for the forgiveness of our sins. He is Holy and just and must punish sin, yet He loves us and wants us to live in heaven forever with Him.

Jesus said, "I am the way the truth and the life, no man cometh unto the Father but by me." (John 14:6)

The only way Jesus can affect our lives is for us to receive Him. "As many as received Him, to them gave he power to become the sons of God, even to them that believe on His name." (John 1:12)

We must repent of our sin, "Repent ye therefore, and be converted, that your sins be blotted out." (Acts 3:19) and turn to God, and place your faith in Jesus, "For by grace are you saved through faith, and that not of yourselves; it is the gift of God." (Ephesians 2:8)

Surrender to Jesus as Lord, by faith, "If thou shalt confess with thy mouth the Lord Jesus, and shalt believe in thine heart that God hath raised Him from the dead, thou shalt be saved. For with the heart man believeth unto righteousness, and with the mouth confession is made unto salvation." (Romans 10:9-10)

"Whosoever shall call upon the name of the Lord shall be saved." (Romans 10:13)

If you want to ask Jesus to save you, please pray this prayer:

Dear God, I know that Jesus is Your Son, and that He died on the cross to pay the price for my sin, and that He rose from the dead. I know I have sinned and need forgiveness. I am willing to turn from my sins and receive Jesus as my Savior and Lord. Thank you for saving me. In Jesus name, Amen.

If you sincerely prayed this prayer, the Lord heard and answered you. You are now a child of God and will spend your eternity with Him. You have just made the most important decision of your life! Welcome to the family of God! I encourage you to find a church that will teach you more about who God is and the inheritance that you will receive as His child! God bless you!

About the Author

GAIL COLEMAN grew up in a small town in Kansas and married her high school sweetheart, Chris Coleman. They had their first child, Brandon, while they were juniors in high school and chose to marry and make a home and family. Three years later they had their daughter, Renelle, and soon thereafter they learned that Jesus Christ died for their sins. They chose to trust Him as their Savior and received the forgiveness that He gives to all who believe.

Prairie Lakes Photography

Chris gave his life to ministry and together they worked in bi-vocational ministry in three different small towns for a total fifteen years. Gail homeschooled their children, starting when Brandon was in the first grade, all the way through to their senior years. She also coached high school volleyball and assisted with girls' high school basketball for the home school league and also a private school.

Following Brandon's accident, she became his main caregiver for seven years. Once he achieved independence, she worked as an administrative assistant, an engineering secretary, a manufacturing engineering tech, and an executive assistant. None of these positions could even hold a candle to the rewarding and fulfilling job of being a wife, mother, caregiver, homemaker, and domestic engineer.

Her hobbies include, crocheting, cross-stitching, interior decorating, and gardening.

You can email her at amothersknot@hotmail.com or visit her website www.amothersknot.com.